STRATEGIES FOR SUCCESSFUL TEACHING
IN URBAN SCHOOLS:

IDEAS AND TECHNIQUES FROM
CENTRAL CITY TEACHERS

by

Gordon L. Berry

Published by

R & E RESEARCH ASSOCIATES, INC.
Publishers
936 Industrial Avenue
Palo Alto, California 94303

Library of Congress Card Catalog Number
81-84973

I.S.B.N.
0-88247-642-4(Hardcover)
0-88247-632-7(Softcover)

Teacher, come on outside! I'll race you to the seesaw!
No, you won't fall off! I'll show you how! Don't be
afraid, teacher. Grab my hand and follow me. You can
learn all over again! . . .(Cullum, 1973)

TABLE OF CONTENTS

PREFACE

The information presented in this handbook was part of a larger national study conducted a number of years ago on teacher training and teaching in the urban or inner city schools. The study was under the direction of Contemporary Research Incorporated (CRI) and the U. S. Office of Education. Its general purpose was to identify the most prevalent problems faced by experienced inner city teachers, and to compare them with those problems faced by teachers who were especially prepared to work in urban schools. Equally important to the study was the desire to have both groups of teachers identify the techniques or strategies they employed to handle the problems they faced.

I was associated with CRI during the period of this study and have subsequently maintained some contact with its former president, Mr. William McAdoo. He and I felt that there were important elements of the original study that had practical implications for urban teachers and administrators today.

I have prepared this book as a type of guide for those professional teachers, administrators and other support personnel who work in urban schools. In doing so, I have taken many liberties in terms of shaping the content so that it could be practical and functional.

The reader will note that many of the techniques and suggestions are often presented verbatim just as the teachers reported to the researchers who interviewed them. In this regard, you may not agree with the problems identified and the strategies or techniques they employed to handle them. I trust, however, that those of you who work in or are concerned with urban school teachers will study some of the techniques and see if they might form a springboard for your own professional activity.

I should like to express my appreciation to William McAdoo for keeping me involved in this project over the years. I would certainly like to note the fine drawings created by Keith Miller. Special thanks

vii

should also go to Robin Greene for some of the secondary research work, and to Juanita Berry for sharing with me her keen insight into teaching strategies for children in urban schools.

Finally, a number of researchers and staff people were originally associated with this project. I must, however, take the responsibility for modifying their initial research efforts in order to design the material for functional use by educators in the schools.

Gordon L. Berry

CHAPTER I

INTRODUCTION

TEACHING IN OUR INNER-CITY SCHOOLS:
CHALLENGES AND PROMISES

Teaching in the large urban schools today can be rewarding, trying, good, bad, and at all times stimulating. Whatever the situation or condition, most of us who have taught in this setting would agree that the experience offers great challenge and much promise. The thrust of the challenge is that our inner-city or urban communities are dynamic environments composed of families with a multiplicity of economic, social, and psychological needs which compete with the school for the hearts and minds of its children. Thus, the urban child, regardless of race, is often caught in a maze of these societal situations that stimulate behaviors which are not rewarded nor clearly understood in the school. And yet, given the lifestyle of the child and his or her parents, their actions and behaviors may be reasonable responses to the way in which they perceive their environment.

It is important to note that to describe the urban environment as composed of certain dynamic elements is not to presuppose that they are all negative and destructive. Indeed, the promise of these communities is that they have a rich cultural base from which they can draw support and innately intelligent people who have, in spite of great odds, been able to master many of the major hurdles of the larger society. In addition, this is also a community where the parents and the adults believe in the potential of the school and education as a way of improving their lives. And yet, the school has not been able to capitalize on the dynamic strengths of the community, or to convince the people that it is willing to blend its skill and knowledge with theirs in a cooperative attempt to provide a quality educational program for the children.

This study, which is the subject of this handbook, was conducted by Contemporary Research Incorporated (CRI) for the Office of Economic Opportunity and Office of Education, and was one attempt to get a picture of the interactions taking place within inner-city schools from the perspective of the classroom teacher. Such a perspective is extremely important because past and present studies support the notion that the teacher and his or her attitudes and behavior toward the child have a great impact on how the child will progress in a school setting.

In order for the reader to better understand the full structure and style of the material to be presented in subsequent chapters of this book, a brief overview of the research design for the initial study will be discussed. First, the CRI staff selected eight national teacher training programs which met the following requirements of the study design:

1. Program contained a major preservice component.

2. Program contained components oriented toward inner-city teaching.

3. Program prepares teachers for elementary schools.

4. Program has sufficient number of graduates, currently teaching in inner-city elementary schools close to the program location, who have taught for five years or less.

At each site, project staff arranged interviews with teachers who were graduates of the selected "exemplary" program and with the directors of each program. CRI staff also arranged interviews at all sites with "peer" teachers on the basis of the following criteria:

1. must have taught five years or less.

2. must *not* be a graduate of preservice training program identified as "exemplary."

3. must be presently teaching in an inner-city school within the same school district as program graduates.

The total study group size was 248 drawn from seven cities throughout the United States. There were 125 graduates of recommended programs and 123 peer teachers in the sample.

The CRI staff developed two instruments for interviews of selected graduate and peer teachers. Project staff administered a questionnaire and interviewed teachers and program directors. Both questionnaires listed 50 problems previously identified by inner-city teachers in Los Angeles, California. These problems related to the six general areas of:

Problem Area A: Relations with Parents and Community

Problem Area B: Instruction and learning

Problem Area C: Colleague and school staff

Problem Area D: Relations with administration

Problem Area E: Inadequacy of resources

Problem Area F: Affective classroom management

Information from directors and related data were contained in the total report. However, the focus of this handbook was on the responses of the teachers.

The questionnaire presented the 50 problems to the teachers in random fashion. The teachers were requested to rate the prevalence of each problem in their school and to deal with each problem.

The staff administered an interview to the teachers immediately following completion of the questionnaire. For each problem where the teacher responded as being currently "competent," or "very competent" to deal with, the interviewer asked the teacher to explain the specific methods used in handling the problem. The interview next asked the teacher which specific aspects of his or her training program were most helpful.

Summarizing the research design for greater clarity, we find that 248 teachers were chosen who had been teaching no longer than five years. Half of them were graduates of eight highly recommended teacher training programs with major components designed specifically to prepare teachers for inner-city elementary schools. The other half were "peer" teachers teaching in elementary schools in the same school district as these graduates.

4

These teachers were then asked by the CRI staff about the prevalence of specific problems in their school and their competence to handle them. When the teachers said they felt competent to deal with a prevalent problem, they were then asked to describe the strategies and techniques they *actually* used to handle these problems. In the full report of the study, CRI quantified selected differences in the responses of the "peer teachers" and "graduates." The author chose not to make such a distinction in the first seven chapters of this book because the essential objective was to share with the reader the techniques these teachers reported using when they felt competent to handle specific problems. The last chapter does present summary strategies and techniques from the major findings and trends.

The reader should understand along with the research design that many of the techniques are often presented verbatim, just as the teachers reported them to the interviewer. In this regard, you may not agree with the techniques offered by the teachers in the study. Indeed, some of the techniques are not those you might use in handling problems. Therefore, the results of applying such techniques in a classroom or the rationale behind their use were not the intent of the initial study, nor an objective of this particular handbook. It was the objective of this book to bring some visibility to the problems, strategies, and techniques utilized by some inner-city teachers so that all interested persons could review them, evaluate them, compare them with their own, and perhaps to begin to develop some grassroots and *meaningful* dialogue concerning the teaching learning process in our schools.

Several final caveats relate to a need for us to return to an initial premise concerning the challenges and promises of teacher in our urban schools. It would, of course, be naive for any of us to romanticize a type of teaching which is truly demanding. However, all "good" teaching whether it is an urban or suburban environment is demanding and at times difficult.

The real truth of the matter is that we are faced in our schools today with an ever changing population of children, a greater demand by community groups seeking to have a voice, and pressure from the courts and government agencies to carry out certain mandates of the law. If those of us in teaching and the total field of education are going to meet the challenge of these changing times, it will be necessary for us to improve the educational program so that inner-city children can have a productive educational experience. This means, for educators, that we must recognize a new relationship with the community in the development of the educational enterprise. It also means that we will have to pursue *excellence without compromise* for the urban child (Berry, 1973). For too long, we have asked urban children and those of the underclass to tolerate a disadvantaged curriculum which has not tapped their untapped potentials.

It would be remiss of the author to close this section without commenting on the serious attempts from capable and dedicated teachers presently working in our inner-city schools. Indeed, many of the techniques which are included in this handbook have grown out of concern for the children, and a sincere attempt to help them toward a full and productive life. When we see and hear of these sensitive and concerned teachers, we realize that the challenges facing our inner-city schools are not impossible to meet, and there are some educators who are serious about doing their part toward working for a rational, productive, and humanistic reconstruction of the inner-city school.

CHAPTER II

PARENT AND COMMUNITY PROBLEMS

Parents living in the central city and the school personnel who teach their children often find that there is a large gap between their views concerning the educational process. Generally speaking, the parents want their children to receive a "good education" and believe that the school is a vehicle for upward mobility. Teachers and administrators, on the other hand, are often critical of parents because they feel there could be more support and understanding for the school program coming from the home.

The public translation of the gap between the community and the school is that parents feel the teachers are insensitive and disinterested in their children, and there is a clear need for more community control. The school personnel suggest that many of the problems they face in the school are present because the parents do not or cannot instill the value of education in their children, and this is reflected in the poor attendance patterns, behavior problems and inadequate work habits.

The teachers in this study clearly reflected the feeling that many of their school problems were related to the child's lifestyle at home as well as those in the general community. Teacher strategies for working with their problems ranged all the way from feeling that they must learn to live with the home conditions to working directly with parents and community agencies.

The problem areas identified by the teachers were:

1. The parents are unable to help their children with school-work because they, themselves, may have lacked some

educational opportunities.

2. The community wants to control the school but lacks the knowledge to make viable school policy.

3. The community has been allowed to deteriorate because of inadequate city services.

4. The neighborhood is dangerous because of a great deal of crime and drug traffic.

5. Parents often don't have the resources to feed and clothe their children adequately.

6. Parents appear to distrust and are hostile toward the school and especially toward middle class teachers.

7. Parents are uninterested in their children's work at school.

8. My values and background are very different from those of the community and therefore understanding and communication between myself and community members are lacking.

9. Parents' dialect or language is different from standard English which hinders pupil performance.

10. The isolation of the school from the community deprives pupils of learning from resources within the community.

The ten problem areas identified above represent the broad concerns from teachers in the field. A more detailed analysis of inner-city's teachers' perceptions of these problems and their suggestions for handling them are discussed in the remainder of the chapter.

PROBLEM: The parents are unable to help their children with schoolwork because they lacked educational opportunity.

STRATEGIES:
1.   Teacher contacts parents by notes or phone:

Techniques Reported For This Strategy

Teacher instructs parents how to help child by sending home notes to parents that explain the homework, subject, project, with exact instructions on what is to be done. Parents given materials to work with at home, weekly readers, weekly schedule. Explain simply in writing how it can help. Send home study kits. Send letters home at beginning of year so parents will expect homework and when, and will be expected to help child with homework. Teacher sends home her home phone number so parents can call about homework assignments.

Teacher encourages parents to do generally supportive education for their children such as listening to child read, spend time with the child; e.g., 15 minutes a day.

Communication with parents: phone parents, make parent aware of problem and ask for help, tell parents to call or write and ask questions.

2.   Teacher meets personally with parents:

Teacher goes to see parent: visit parents at home, set up study centers in homes and times for children to study at home, work with parents individually at home, show them how best to help.

Teacher invites parents into classroom: conferences at school with parents; ask parent to come into the classroom and help out; explain at beginning of semester to parents what class would be doing; ask them to come in and watch kids work; instruct parents in classroom on what to do; use of games (Miami linguistics series) by teacher to involve both parent and child; all parents come in three times a year; invite them to get workbooks; open classroom.

Teacher involves parents in a learning experience of their own; workshops for parents; find out from Board of Education what educational programs or materials are available for parents; encourage them to go back to school; tutor parents for own classes; make parents feel competent to help.

Have parent assistance club; organize parents into groups which meet every two weeks and teach them how to teach; examine textbooks; reivew work and hear speakers and films and do sample of homework.

3. Teacher depends upon student:

Design work so parents don't have to help; make sure it is things they can do at home.

Encourage children to use their own resources; let those able to work independently; have children read to their parents; use some other child (brother or sister) as tutors in same apartment building; have better students help poorer ones; cross-age tutoring; cross-achievement tutoring; use older students from nearby private schools as tutors; tell children to go straight home and do homework before it gets too crowded or noisy.

Teacher works with child in classroom during school hours: child will do most of his homework in class; gets extra help in classroom; more individual attention; all work at school— or only limited amount of homework at home; extra drills in class; homework center for those who can't do it at home.

After school tutoring.

Grouping in rooms: use centers in rooms; use grouping for slower learners.

4. Teacher utilizes resource people:

Resource people, coordinating instructor, paraprofessionals, student teachers, community workers, history students, university field workers, if language is a problem, get bilingual aide.

5. Other teacher strategies:

Send extra work home.

Have record of homework turned in to show parents.

Advise parents not to help; do not want them to help.

Explain to parents the need to encourage child; withdraw privileges; see that time is spent on homework.

Send note home asking them if they want child to have homework.

Keep math homework for school time; just let spelling and reading go home.

Try to make parents understand they have absolutely no obligation to help if they cannot.

PROBLEM: The community wants to control the school but lacks the knowledge to make viable school policy.

STRATEGIES:
1. Teacher involves parents, community groups:

Techniques Reported For This Strategy

Meet with parents to discuss parent/leader roles.

Talk, write, phone parents to interest them and give support and understanding.

Have parent workshops, discussions, meetings; even in summer.

Take informal and formal polls on what parents would like to see happen.

Work through county aides, politicians, community groups.

Get parents involved in federal reading program; try to organize a small school board; make visits to parents' home.

Get parents, community leaders, teacher from Parent Action Committee to work with problems.

Encourage parents to attend and support PTA.

Respond to parent grievances, questions of school policy, etc.

Parents go to community board with grievances (e.g., teachers/school).

Remove child from class when parents disagree with policy.

Elected board holds "block" meetings to acquaint parents with board.

Set up rules and regulations beginning of year to let parents know my plan for achievement.

Employ role play techniques during parent workshops.

2.   Other strategies:

Try to avoid problem.

Get administration, principal, vice principals, etc. involved in community problems.

Live in community; play both roles.

Convey my positive attitude for community to administration.

Respond to questions of paraprofessionals preparing to be teachers.

PROBLEM: The community has been allowed to deteriorate because of inadequate city services.

STRATEGIES:

1. Teacher assumes responsibility:

   Techniques Reported For This Strategy

   Had school newspaper with parents column telling who to contact for certain problems.

   Have own physical education/games program—makes up for playground deterioration.

   Don't use community facilities.

   Attend and speak up at community meetings, PTA.

2. Teacher involves students:

   Encourage student cleanliness and personal safety at school and home.

   Special projects developed through class participation: block campaign, pocket park, letter drive.

   Encourage student to keep school/block/area/community clean.

   Discuss problem of pollution in relation to community deterioration.

   Encourage pupils to take pride in what they have in the community.

3. Teacher involves parents, community:

   Belong to community groups.

   Tell parents how to find social services (e.g., housing, social workers, community action groups).

   Support local officials in their complaints about inadequate city services.

   Attend parent/teacher/community meetings to discuss

14

school/neighborhood problems.

4. Other strategies:

Don't let it bother me.

Deterioration makes area unsafe—class doesn't go out; I go out of community; won't live here.

Live with it; not afraid to go to work.

Address personal complaints at community meeting.

PROBLEM: The neighborhood is dangerous because of a great deal of crime and drug traffic.

STRATEGIES:
1. Teacher's personal approach:

Techniques Reported For This Strategy

Learned to live with it.

Lock all doors and don't stay after school.

Attend college level courses on subject of drugs.

Try to understand that students have to live under these pressures.

2. Teacher involves students:

Advise students not to be on streets at night with money.

Advise students not to talk to strangers.

Discuss movies and tell stories about neighborhood and school crime in class; discuss city laws.

Discourage drug use; discuss and have films.

PTA and school board work with pupils and design programs

supplying drug information.

Deal with urban affairs via social studies.

Visit juvenile center.

Get kids together as friends in school.

Have problem-solving sessions based on kids' experiences.

Discuss possibility of being sold candy with something in it.

Let kids out early.

Walk or drive kids home.

Make kids aware of what is right and wrong.

Discuss necessity of education and technical education so kids can better themselves and leave the ghetto.

3. Teacher involves parents:

    PTA works with parents giving drug information.

    Talk to parents about their involvement in school.

    Have parents pick up their children after school.

4. Teacher and the administration:

    PTA meetings held in afternoon due to low evening turnout because of crime in area.

    Refer serious cases involving drugs or theft to administration (principal, counselor, etc.)

5. Teacher involves community:

    Get community involved (e.g., community meetings).

    Call police after burglary.

Have meetings and talk with community leaders.

Support an education council; have parent/neighborhood watch.

Live in community; have common lifestyle.

Have county people in to talk on drugs, crime, etc. (police, ex-addict).

6.   Other strategies:

Draw from own experiences in dealing with community.

Teach kids responsibility for own actions.

Discourage violence.

Look at who is walking around school.

Point out negative aspects of urban life.

PROBLEM: Parents don't always have the resources to feed and clothe their children adequately.

STRATEGIES:
1.   Teacher involves parents:

Techniques Reported For This Strategy

Let parents know about job opportunities.

Make suggestions about job opportunities.

Inform parents that problem exists.

Contact parent; call and/or write to see if we can help or if they would be offended if we did.

Let parent know of available programs.

Check with parents to see if children are fed.

Provide model: room mother assists during lunch or nutrition hour; room mother plans Christmas party.

Go into home and try to help child.

Notify parents that free breakfast is available.

Don't let children's appearance bother me as much since I know them personally.

2. Teacher involves students, students assume some responsibility:

Kids bring in food and clothes as class projects.

Teach children to mend tears and sew on buttons.

Get them to wear what they have and keep clean.

3. Teacher discusses, explains:

Encourage children to eat breakfast and lunch.

Encourage child to eat vegetables at night, not sweets.

Have health lessons on what foods to eat every day and why.

Have a lesson on how to clean your own clothes.

Discuss in class what is possible for them to have now; talk about problems.

Have class discussions regarding tolerance, people's feelings, and that the way people dress is irrelevant to the worth of a person.

Talk about keeping neat and taking care of what you have; take pride in what you are.

Do hygiene program in class.

4. Teacher involves community, agencies:

Refer problem to certain community agencies.

Rely on people in community development programs.

Distribute donated items from religious institutions.

Refer family to proper agency or place.

Depend on community liaison.

Follow up with agency after referral.

Ask stores to donate.

All in community donate clothes.

5. Teacher involves other teachers, administration:

Refer to PTA.

Refer to consultant.

Refer to guidance counselor.

Refer to principal/office; they contact parent.

Work or refer through social service worker.

Arranged for afternoon snack to replace free breakfast as my kids are fed breakfast at home.

School has free lunch and breakfast program.

School has a food center set up by a volunteer program.

School has a shoe fund and provides shoes.

School has a clothes closet, clothing.

Refer to nurse.

School provides emergency lunch passes.

Arrange for free lunches and send in extra lunch ticket.

Refer or take kids to school/parent coordinator; pupil personnel workers.

Paraprofessionals and aides take care of it; collect used clothes and distribute.

Call community assistant (at school).

School is in Follow Through program funded by federal government which allots money for clothes.

Refer to visiting teacher.

Truant officer may deliver clothes in home.

Refer to Follow Through nurse who goes into home.

Teachers bring clothes and toys children can buy.

Have yearly clothing drive.

6. Teacher assumes responsibility:

Get help from relatives.

Get clothes from other people and give to children.

Make repairs myself (resole shoes).

Students without coats don't go outside on a cold day.

Try to fill in as a parent.

I've gotten emergency food orders for desperate family.

Have made approintments with parents and picked up their commodity foods.

Don't ridicule what students wear to class.

Don't treat children any differently.

Donate clothes to school's facility.

Get uneaten lunches left from 1st grade class and give to my children (get two lunches).

Have modeling class for girls after school; they fix own hair, makeup.

Keep oranges in my desk for the kids; have clothing in room for them.

7. General statements:

See parents informally; they know I'm available.

Don't make a case out of it.

Take steps to correct problems with food and clothes.

By telling myself that by teaching the child as much as I can, he can hopefully make it out of ghetto and provide for himself.

PROBLEM: Parents distrust and are hostile toward the school and class teachers.

STRATEGIES:
1. Teacher's personal approach toward parent:

Techniques Reported For This Strategy

Accept them as they are, don't put on airs or talk like a know-it-all; treat as equals.

Be friendly to parents.

Show I'm on their side (for parents, community); show I'm interested, concerned.

Don't worry about it; not afraid.

Stay out of parents' way.

Indicate it's a privilege to teach their child; that I'm there for their child; will work very hard for them.

Listen to what they have to say; respect their ideas.

Give them red carpet treatment.

Try to make myself helpful (with tact).

Don't argue with parent hostile to discipline.

2. Teacher visits parent's home:

Make home visits, at the beginning of each semester.

Make home visits within approved school policy.

Feels free to visit at any time.

Walk home with child and stay and talk.

3. Teacher's techniques:

Involve parent as volunteer in class.

Ask parents to help when child is in trouble.

Involve parents in tutoring sessions.

Organize parents at beginning of year to participate in class.

Have parent conferences.

Contact parents by phone or personal visit.

Send home notes or letters inviting parental participation.

Ask parents to call me at home.

Let parents know what we're doing; how to help.

Keep parents informed of child's progress throughout year.

Let parents know I consider teaching their child a big responsibility that I couldn't handle without their help.

Encourage parents to discuss their expectations; be more involved.

See parents at PTA.

Let parents unload before I say anything.

Talk straight to parent; deal with facts.

Try to come through on what I promise.

Let parent know we are both working for same goal.

Tell them I'm always available for any reason.

Follow up with note after contacting parent.

Give parent positive reinforcement and praise child's good grades to establish rapport.

Ask for parents' opinion or advice regarding discipline.

Try to be honest and open about child to parent.

Discuss what I expect of child with parent.

Assure them child is not being taken out of his environment.

Issue weekly comments on how much of a study or behavior contract is completed.

Explain situation to parent when child tries to get you in trouble and have child present at discussion; show all being treated equally.

Keep anecdotal records of problem children with witnesses, dates, and times.

4.   Teacher invites parents to school:

For parties and field trips, fun night.

Have open classroom policy which encourages parent to visit.

Have an open house at beginning of year to discuss mutual expectations or meet with them individually.

Request for parents to visit via report cards.

5. Teacher involves student:

Let children do research on the problem of distrust and hostility toward authority.

Work on individual basis with child in special need.

Be affectionate with children.

6. Teacher involves community:

Attend meetings, community events (build up trust).

Get out into community and make field trips.

Attend workshops at Human Relations Department.

Visit community centers and talk with people who work there.

7. Teacher involves other teachers, administration:

Let principal act as buffer.

Become a member of human relations cadre in district.

Attend workshops.

Have special club or program at school.

Parent conference with principal and teacher.

Have and use paraprofessional liaison.

Suggest to teachers that they attend community functions.

Encourage principal to have activities (chaperones to baseball games).

Inform principal of any action taken.

When hostility expressed physically, call in assistant principal.

Seek advice from those who live in community and can tell you of a pupils' situation.

8. Other strategies:

Don't touch pupils of hostile parents.

Make self free at parent's convenience at school.

Take kids places on weekends (museum) or to my home.

Have parents to my home.

If parents wants child removed from class, I oblige.

Rely on past experience of similar situations.

Send materials home when different.

9. General statements:

Try to reassure parents.

One's own personality and attitude is important to increase trust.

Try not to be middle class.

I'm active in groups dealing with parents and students.

Get parents interested; work with both parent and child.

Try to start good relationships at beginning of year.

They see I have expectations and they are more cooperative.

PROBLEM: Parents are uninterested in their children's work at school.

STRATEGIES:
1. Teacher involves parents:

Techniques Reported For This Strategy

Explain to parent what I am trying to do and what child's problems are; send home letters or notes.

Point out that parental interest in schoolwork is a form of interest in their child and they should be involved in this process.

Express need for parents to reinforce what is learned in school.

Send home papers including test papers with notes, have parents sign and return them.

Show parents their child can succeed.

Meet, contact, and telephone parents.

Send child's work home in folder with interesting comment praising child for effort.

Present child as having lots of possibilities and try to make parents see their responsibilities toward childrearing.

Follow up contact if parent says he will help.

Send progress reports home in addition to report card.

Try to give positive feedback and buildup.

Find out about family situation and transfer similarities between school and home to the family.

Send things home; not just schoolwork.

Send note home when we go from one book to another.

Keep folders of each child's work for parents to see.

Corner parents at school functions.

Show or send home positive work child has done.

Send home excellent work to be signed.

Send easy work to take home to make parent think he really helped.

2. Teacher visits parents:

Make home visit.

Explain what is to be accomplished.

Go and show positive attitude.

3. Teacher invites parents to school:

Teachers generally invite parents.

Invite for parent/teacher conferences.

For workshops at school's classes.

For special programs or activities.

To observe, work with me, see progress of child.

For informal afternoon coffee session.

4. Teacher involves parent, parent assumes some responsibility:

Instruct parents how to use materials I send home.

Tell parent how to develop own materials using things in the home.

Ask parents for suggestions, opinions.

Have them volunteer for art or after school tutoring.

Ask parents to write comment on papers sent home; sign daily report.

Get parents to see kids actually do work.

Read with child; ask questions.

Tell parents to have children show them work; talk about school; hang up work, use it.

Parent is to do one assignment with child.

Give homework parents must help with.

5. Teacher involves student, student assumes some responsibility:

Child corrects parents' homework (assumes teacher role).

Must have parents sign failing papers.

Fulfill contracts and group discussions.

Encourage them to get older brothers and sisters to help.

Pupils take work home and explain it to parents.

Students are to ask parents for information about subjects.

Children have stories to read to parents.

Send out sets of alphabet letters with each child.

Kids encourage parents to attend school functions.

Tell kids to take work home and put it up (e.g., tape on refrigerator).

Have special projects children can share with parents.

Have behavior reward system in class.

Get parents interested by making children feel parent should be interested.

Have kids take pictures of home and parents; make into book that kids take home.

6.   Teacher's techniques:

Give homework occasionally.

Assign homework in folders.

Give lots of homework.

Try to make homework fun; I mimeograph it.

Use relatives to reinforce students.

Have special message stamp to use on their papers.

Develop kids' self-reliance by telling them they can do anything—they're special.

Use peer group influence.

Reward good behavior.

Deal with child on his ability level, not supposed grade level.

7.   Teacher involves other teachers, administration:

Have administration contact parents I can't reach.

School has parents night once a month.

Assistant principal contacts parents who don't respond to form letter.

Work through paraprofessionals who speak to parents.

Principal/teacher conferences.

8. Other strategies:

Hang work around school for people to see.

Bring kids into my home on weekends.

Help children after school; give special attention.

Encourage child to do best he can; praise child; try to give him self-confidence.

Let child know I'm concerned, but I don't take over a parent.

9. General statement:

Try to sell myself to parents.

Assume that parents are interested.

Show interest and concern; treat each child differently.

Establish rapport.

Offer positive suggestions.

Try to get them involved in school programs.

Try to be friendly.

Get children to respect and trust me.

Have kids interested in what they do in school.

PROBLEM: My values and background are very different from those of community and therefore understanding and communication between myself and community members are lacking.

STRATEGIES:
1. Teacher advises those who find this a problem:

30

Sort out values which are universal.

Try to forget own values; accept/respect theirs.

Spend lots of time in community (evenings, weekends, etc.); businesses, parents, with people.

Try to be more of a listener than talker to kids/parents.

Am interested in kids and try to do a good job.

Grew up in community/live here.

Parents respect teachers who try despite background.

Bring pupils' backgrounds into class; foods; rap sessions.

Talk to other teachers, counselors about parents/problems.

Take students on field trips.

Make home visits to student homes.

Try to find out parents' expectations of me and meet them.

My purpose is to make child feel good about self.

Learn from kids; their experiences, lifestyles, community.

Make friends in the community.

Become aware of problems that exist, self-evaluation, self-education.

Rely on previous experience in the inner-city (social, work, autonomy, counselor, etc.).

Never make home visits out of fear.

Talk to parents at start/throughout school year.

Bring food/snacks in for hungry children.

Accepting/understanding but not judging (e.g., do not push standard English usage).

Stay after school with kids.

Involve parents in class activities.

Share economic background of most parents.

2. Teachers personally find it a problem:

Relate to child as child.

Find out needs of child.

Gain understanding through paraprofessionals from community.

Go to administration, guidance, health personnel for pupil/parent problems.

Try to involve parents at school (PTA, community, etc.).

Get involved in PTA, community functions.

Communicate with parents: notes, phone calls, weekly reports about the child's school/social, etc., behavior.

3. Other strategies:

Try to overcome general feeling the faculty has towards the community.

Ignore faculty paranoia.

Learn much by keeping eyes and ears open.

PROBLEM: Parents' dialect or language is different from standard English would hinder pupil performance.

STRATEGIES:

1. Teacher involves parents:

    Techniques Reported For This Strategy

    Ask parents to use English at home.

    Respect parents' dialect.

    Encourage parents to take adult ESL.*

    Speak Spanish to parents and send notes in Spanish.

    Make home visits to parents.

    Tell parents what we are doing in class.

2. Teacher involves students, students assume some responsibility:

    Kids help me talk to parents (i.e., language barrier).

    Peers help each other with work.

    Have bilingual child translate.

    Use siblings to tutor child in English.

    Hold class discussions.

3. Teacher involves other teachers, administration:

    Work with and use paraprofessionals, aides, and ESL teacher who know other languages/Spanish.

    Use translator.

    Bilingual program at school.

    See speech consultant regarding speech impediments.

---

*English as a Second Language curriculum.

Put child in ESL program.

Have programmed audio language classes.

Give auditory discrimination tests to children.

4. Teacher's personal approach:

Make kids aware of dialect differences.

I have learned words in different languages.

Encourage peer interaction; helps children pick up English through group activity.

I am example for them (standard English).

Kids need both school and street/home dialect: stress standard English in class, but say that nonstandard is okay for playground and community; make them bilingual.

Encourage kids to talk and don't correct them or demean them when they do talk/use dialect.

Accept children's dialect; don't let it bother me.

Impress upon child that he or she use the right word in class.

Learn black dialect.

Teach Spanish in class.

Use Spanish in class.

Build up a child's confidence in how he speaks.

Explain to children why it is important for them to learn English, for tests and for later life.

5. Teacher's techniques:

Appeal primarily to visual communication.

Define new words for students.

Clap out sound of words with hands.

Use choral or oral singing technique.

Stress awareness of pronunciation.

Stress verbal communication in class.

Say it their way (slang), then demonstrate school based English patterns.

Make special work for non-English students in class.

Offer alternative ways of saying things.

Start lessons in simple terms or words; use words meaningful to them.

Correct their English.

Stress standard English in lessons.

Make sure children understand instructions.

Have them answer me using complete sentences.

Use stories and poems; tell stories.

Study parts of speech and their use in class.

Have grammar lessons.

Use phonetics as a teaching tool.

Develop word attack skills.

Use language experience approach.

Use language models.

Use creative writing approach.

Encourage repetition of new words.

Use learning centers highlighting standard English.

Use oral reading to class as often as possible.

Encourage kids to get library cards and check out books.

Other techniques used: demonstrate new words, role play, stress word endings, tailor/prepare lessons, speak slowly, illustrate, individualize, let children talk while they are working, give speaking parts in plays, say or draw the word.

6. Teacher's materials:

    Make own materials that will aid instruction.

    Use tape recorders, tapes, and newspapers.

7. Other strategies:

    Encourage other people to come into class.

    Take a linguistic theory course in college.

    Go to a training program to improve dialect skills.

PROBLEM: The isolation of the school from the community deprives pupils of learning from resources within the community.

STRATEGIES:
1. Teacher and class go into community or learn about community and world events:

    Techniques Reported For This Strategy

    Take field trips as far away as possible: museums, parks, zoos, in country.

    Take field trips to community agencies: police, health and fire departments.

Get out of classroom; give them new experiences.

Have weekend activities, parties.

Use books, films, TV to introduce outside world.

Develop lessons around class trips.

Open school to community.

Have social studies unit conducted at local medical center.

Have children bring in things from their environment.

Take pictures with kids on community walks.

Class participates in community activities.

Talk about good role models from their racial or ethnic group, using well-known people.

Inform students of current community resources, events, improvement measures.

Talk about situation in the school before integration.

2. Teachers get resources from community:

Call on specially skilled parents/people to share these skills with kids.

Kids talk to class about their father's work.

Open invitation to all parents to visit, help out (volunteers), attend workshops, socials.

Businesses willing to cooperate with talks, visits, facilities, etc.

Parents offer advice and solutions for understanding of kids.

Have community people in to visit classroom: Red Cross, merchants, agency representatives.

Check out books from public library for kids' use.

3.   Other strategies:

Encourage parents to attend PTA.

Call to see what trips are available.

Kids put on slide show for parents.

Have my students tutor younger ones in school.

Draw maps of community, neighborhood.

The challenge to both parents and teacher is great because any gulf between the two groups must be bridged if together they are to have a meaningful impact on the education of the child. The inner-city child has the capacity to do well in school based on his or her competencies. Unfortunately, the child must compete with a multiplicity of other forces which can impede progress toward attaining full potential. Thus the issue is not to point a finger at the home or school but to see how they can mutually work together in order to serve the child. This section has clearly identified the perceptions of a group of teachers working in the central city. Some of the problems and strategies for working with them have value for you as a teacher in the school, and others leave a great deal to be desired in terms of workable approaches.

What is important is for those of us in education to continue with our efforts to meaningfully involve parents in school activities so that the education of children can become a cooperative undertaking to be shared by both. Pellegrino (1973) suggested that parents have a right and a responsibility to be informed about what is happening in the schools and to be aware of constructive means which they may actively employ in being of service to their children and their schools. Teachers also have the right to expect that parents will assist them in carrying out the instructional program insofar as the conduct of the child is concerned.

Parent and teacher involvement and cooperation does not just happen. They both take commitment and leadership on the part of the two groups. The strategy to seek is one where there can be continuous interaction with the goal of helping each child develop to his or her greatest potential.

CHAPTER III

INSTRUCTION AND LEARNING PROBLEMS

A great deal of attention has been directed toward those issues related to the instructional and learning problems of inner-city children. Much of the early work in the fields of instruction and learning tended to focus on the need for the teacher (instructor) to develop specialized methodology for working with a somehow deficient learner (inner-city child). The theory supporting these concepts suggested that the psycho-social problems faced by inner-city children caused them to be limited to the degree that new methodology was needed to fill the large linguistic, mathematical, reading, writing, and even personal conduct skills necessary for them to progress adequately in a school setting.

This "deficit instructional model" for inner-city children brought into the schools a large number of specialized programs which primarily assumed that something was wrong with the cognitive processes of these children and the quality of their home life. As a result, such concepts as stimulus deprivation, arrested learning, and poor auditory discrimination became the "in" words when discussing the teaching-learning process and our inner-city schools. In this connection, Weaver (1972) observed that the deprivation theory placed the burden on the low-income and minority children as well as their families. While it is clear that the inner-city child does come to the school with some problems, we now realize that there are also difficulties with the instructional program of the schools. Thus, the deficiencies frequently referred to as being associated with the children are not remediated by the educational program of the school, but are often reinforced and left to grow until they become an educational way of life for the child.

The teachers in this study identified a number of problems which focused on the child as a learner, and they also pointed out some of the instructional disadvantages in their schools. The teachers also noted problems associated with the physical health of the child and some of the limitations of the environment in which the child must function. Specifically, the most frequently cited problems were as follows:

1. Instructional materials are irrelevant to pupils' cultural background.

2. Too many pupils in the classroom.

3. Classes contain pupils of various ability levels.

4. Pupils are uninterested in school subjects.

5. Pupils have difficulty thinking in abstract terms.

6. Pupils are frequently absent.

7. There is not enough time to plan the curriculum.

8. There is a large percentage of pupil turnover.

9. Pupils have language difficulties.

10. Pupils often achieve below grade norm.

11. Unattended physical problems such as poor eyesight and deafness impede pupils' learning.

12. Pupils have little confidence in their ability to achieve.

The 12 problems of the classroom teachers are reflective of their personal interaction with the children and parents on a daily basis. As each of the above problems reflect that real world view, so will the following strategies that are utilized for coping with them.

PROBLEM: Instructional materials are irrelevant to pupils' cultural background.

STRATEGIES:

1. Teacher doesn't use materials that are irrelevant:

   Techniques Reported For This Strategy

   Put all such materials in closet until June.

   Don't use basal reader.

2. Teacher uses materials but tries to compensate:

   Tell kids that not everyone lives in suburbia.

   Use materials at lower level.

   Use materials but tell kids they're irrelevant.

3. Teacher selectively uses supplied materials:

   Take stories and materials and paraphrase them to fit their experiences.

   Use reading and/or mathematics workbooks, skills sheets.

   Use basal series (Bank Street, Open Highways, Scott Foresman, Harcourt Brace).

   Use ethnic materials on supply in school.

   Use texts only as reference guide.

   Use weekly readers.

   Use what you can get out of texts and materials which is applicable.

   Adapt book materials to environment and background of children.

   Adapt materials to child's level of ability.

42

4. Teacher uses supplementary materials and personnel from outside sources:

   Get material from school supply centers.

   Get material from library.

   Use pamphlets, material, and information put out by organizations and community sources.

   Have people from organizations come into class (community, parents).

   Get materials from workshops I attend.

   Get ideas from teaching journals.

   Ask parents and children for information on their cultures.

   Watch TV shows (Electric Co., science show, ETV).

5. Supplementary activities outside school:

   Kids had recycling of solid waste project in neighborhood.

   Take field trips in community and city.

   Teach in the community and use experience to make materials relevant to students.

6. Students help make or supply materials:

   Children write and make their own books, stories, projects.

   Children bring in articles, pictures, and materials.

   Make weekly newspaper with items that kids write.

   Research in books on black history and put a play together.

   Children suggest what they want to learn.

   Students (with teacher) make packets with puzzles and games.

Students take over school one day (act as teachers and administrators).

7. Teacher makes or supplies materials and lessons:

Write own stories, lessons that are related to children's background.

Bring in materials, audio visuals, and educational aids dealing with famous black people and black heritage.

Make or bring in manipulative visual aids or devices.

Bring in used audio visual materials (records, films, tapes).

Bring in animals.

Use photography (pictures of kids, neighborhood).

Make and bring games for subject areas or related to city life.

Bring in supplies (paper, pencils, stuff for science or art projects).

Make worksheets at their ability level.

Write my own booklets (low reading level but high interest).

Write experience charts, stories.

Bring in magazines (*Jet, Ebony*), books, newspapers.

Use pictures, drawings of minority people.

Make or find my own materials.

Find and bring in ethnic material.

Make up songs about mathematics; use stock market quotations or store prices.

Cut out and use articles (words, pictures) from magazines and newspapers in class.

Have children draw pictures and talk about the city and their homes, experiences.

Kids write plays, stories, and books.

Class makes games/models out of materials they bring into the class.

8. Teacher's techniques:

Give kids camera and let them take pictures of neighborhood and community.

Have students write reports on Malcolm X and other black people.

Send children to the library.

Explain material in simple terms.

Use individualized instruction.

Make daily contracts.

Have centers with materials for different ability levels.

Read a lot to the children.

Use games, songs, activities in lessons.

Take field trips in the immediate community and city to learn about various cultural groups.

Make subjects and activities relate to children's knowledge and experience (map study, own neighborhood, animals, etc.).

Use role play techniques in classroom.

Teach lessons whereby kids can do or see; e.g., make something to eat from the country class is studying.

Ask child what he is interested in and take him to library and pick out books with him.

Stress that they read books dealing with cultural background.

Talk about black, white, Hispanic, Asian and American Indian cultures and how it doesn't hinder friendship.

9. Teacher's curriculum:

    Make up curriculum involving four revolving themes: ecology, community, communication, and economics.

    Teach unit on drugs, sex education, ecology.

    Have an ethnic studies program or center.

    Follow-Through curriculum based on individualized programmed learning: (Singer series) mathematics/manipulative materials; social studies—pictures of inner city; reading (Sullivan series); with reward (token) systems (federally funded program).

10. Teacher's personal approach:

    Tell kids about my experiences regarding social studies topic.

    Do lots of outside reading to get ideas (*Open Classroom*, Herbert Kohl) on subject matter; keep up with current events, TV programs, musical groups.

11. Other strategies:

    Take inservice workshops.

    Borrow or exchange books and ideas from other teachers.

    Convince the district/principal to buy things.

    Tell administrative librarian about irrelevant materials.

12. General statements:

    Use materials that will interest them.

    Make what is necessary.

Make curriculum relevant to the children.

Bring in materials they want to know about.

PROBLEM: Too many pupils in the classroom.

STRATEGIES:
1.   Teacher involves parents, community:

Techniques Reported For This Strategy

Parents come in and work as aides.

Aides from community (high school, college, parents) come in to work with kids.

2.   Teacher involves other teachers, administration:

Use reading teacher.

Aides work with groups.

Employ services of math specialists, student teachers, junior high students, psychologist, and floater teachers.

Faculty formed a minischool/open corridor structure.

Open classroom (four classes, five teachers); subject matter divided among teachers; teach longer than required.

Team teaching situation.

Behavior modification via reward and denial of privileges.

3.   Teacher's techniques:

Group according to ability in reading.

Group according to ability in math.

Group kids according to ability.

47

Grouping based on test results, interest, subject area.

Learning centers in the classroom.

Utilize small group instruction at particular center activity.

Group pupils into varied activities not necessarily by ability.

Individualization: have materials (self-pacing) for fast and slow students while working with whole class.

Teacher-made individualized learning packets.

Work individually with those who need me most.

Sociometric seating (who they want to sit near).

Let child play games or work independently when through with work.

Let faster groups work independently, help each other.

Switch from centers to strict teaching with buddy system.

Instructional techniques include contracts, conferences, activity rotation.

Keep them busy with written and oral work, chalkboard, sharing things.

Seat discipline problems close to my desk or next to those that aren't.

Employ different arrangement to enlarge class size and promote variety: let kids sit on floor, remove my desk, divide up into areas, use extra rooms, semicircles, and arrange desks into groups.

Use workbooks.

Use peers and upper grade students as tutors.

Students correct work themselves.

Use learning games and aids: pictures, filmstrips, flash cards, sequence puzzles, collages, records, transparencies, ABC talking alphabet game, primary typewriter, individualized math kit.

4. Other strategies:

Constantly remind students of need for good behavior; strict disciplinarian; set up standards at beginning of year.

Encourage responsibility, independence, and working together.

PROBLEM: Classes contain pupils of various ability levels.

STRATEGIES:
1. Teacher involves parents:

Techniques Reported For This Strategy

Parents give help at home.

Parents come into class and work with individuals/groups.

Tell parents about before and after school activities that will help their child.

2. Teacher involves students, students assume some responsibility:

Peer tutoring: (both peers) pupils who can't write/read have "secretaries" who know material and get credit for writing what nonwriter dictated.

Employ cross-age tutoring.

Students work independently; make own notebooks, library, trips, journals, stories.

Have children check their own completed work.

Let top group work independently.

Have children write their own stories and books based on their experiences.

Children make their own work contracts.

3. Teacher involves other teachers, personnel, administration:

Tell other teachers to give children work at the level at which they can achieve.

Get help from reading teacher.

Aide works with one of my groups/with individuals.

Get advice from other teachers.

Send some students to other rooms for special help, advanced, or lower ability work.

4. Teacher's techniques:

Let students go into work at higher level if they want.

Praise students for their accomplishments.

Encourage kids to "do their own thing" regarding creative writing, art, reading, etc.

If child finishes ahead of time, can do anything he wants.

Group according to ability level (based on tests).

Group according to ability level in reading.

Group according to ability level in math.

Work individually with child with problem.

Individualization (materials, projects, own rate).

Gear material and work to different levels (from simple to difficult research reports).

Open classroom technique.

See each child one or more times a week regarding reading on individualize basis.

Relate subject to something that affects kids interest (learn graphing with their spelling or street addresses).

Heterogeneous grouping in some or all subjects so slow kids can benefit from fast.

Try and give as much individual attention as possible.

Play games for slower kids.

Keep child after school for private tutoring.

Work in ungraded primary or nongraded class setting.

Nongraded classes.

Teach phonics and linguistics.

Takes lots of trips out into community.

Have learning centers to stimulate interests.

Free school of fixed activities; three fluctuating activities child can choose from.

Use programmed reading curriculum which is individualized.

Before and after school projects and activities geared to various ability levels.

5. Teacher's materials:

Use SRA reading series, weekly reader.

Use Madison Lab math materials, Singer individualized method program.

Made, bought, borrowed library materials.

Newspaper, spare IBM parts, busy box.

Use audio visual and visual aids (records, transparencies, films, tapes, and pictures).

Have independent games, educational aids.

Have manipulative devices that are self-corrective.

Provide special materials for faster kids.

6. Other strategies:

Have team teaching.

Split reading groups between another teacher and myself.

Assign outside reading.

Help students get summer jobs.

7. General statements:

Try and get pupils to respect their honest differences.

Try to meet the ability levels of the children.

PROBLEM: Pupils are uninterested in school subjects.

STRATEGIES:
1. Teacher involves parents:

Techniques Reported For This Strategy

Give parents weekly report.

Write notes home on students who do poorly.

Parents bring in pets from home.

2. Teacher involves student, student assumes some responsibility:

Children make up math games.

Let students be the teacher and teach a lesson on something they have researched.

Let students do independent research on projects they are interested in.

Brighter children conduct games.

Brighter children help slower children.

Children go to the library on their own.

Students decide what they want to study; do it in social studies.

Students give suggestions regarding what they want to do.

Children select academic objectives and goals.

Children write their own topics, books, plays, and bring in costumes, stories, and journals.

Class makes up songs regarding math.

Give freedom to do certain things in classroom.

Free time to work on independent projects.

Divide pupils into interest groups of their creation.

Have students act out events in history, social studies (role playing).

3. Teacher's personal approach:

Be conversant with what is going on in community.

Encourage competition among students; make lesson a game or contest.

Let them experience; find out things on their own; gain independence.

Discuss home problems if they bring them up.

Give attitude to succeed, not fail.

Don't stifle pupils' comments or questions.

Start lessons with jokes, keep children laughing.

Be enthusiastic about what you or they are doing.

Don't push nonreaders to finish series.

Reward or praise if they finish work or do well.

Talk about things I like which are applicable.

4. Teacher's techniques:

    With slower group, switch subjects more often.

    Group reading according to colors so kids can't compare themselves to others.

    Use small groups to decrease teacher-pupil ratio during discussions.

    Change groups daily.

    Interclass activities with another class.

    Have stimulating learning centers.

    Use concrete examples that refer to their families, environmental background, things they are interested in or enjoy (e.g., math, take them to a store, sports, monster shows).

    Set up store in classroom: have children act out puppet parts in the stores, pantomime, role play.

    Take a lot of trips (zoos, farms, aquariums).

Rename school subjects (social studies, pretend we're on a plan trip).

Children act out poems rather than recite.

Take field trips into the community regarding mathematics (store), social studies.

Have ongoing projects in room (growing things, building models).

Children talk, write, and draw about their experiences.

Use a lot of current events for discussion.

Drop some of the uninteresting subjects.

In social studies, teach dances, make costumes, have plays.

Have lots of music for social studies and grammar.

Offer varied program (photography, filming) based on what kids want.

Vary subject matter constantly.

Do experiments in science and have animals in class.

Study drugs, ecology, and crime in their neighborhood; things that affect them in everyday environment.

Use stock quotations to teach mathematics.

Write material about black history for reading or bring in books with ethnic groups in them (e.g., Bank Street reader).

Publish pupils' work in newspaper.

Talk about what interests them, even if nonacademic, and lead into academic.

Use TV programs' (Sesame Street) techniques, words.

Use childrens' names in lessons.

Read a lot of stories to them.

Have extracurricular activities for hyperactive kids (trips, books, art, writing).

Use lesson follow-up games, contests.

Incorporate art, projects, music into lesson.

Give nonreaders prereading skills (reading left to right, tracing) at child's own pace.

Use experiments in science designed to increase participation.

Use a game time with six to ten activities.

Have a grab bag box where students pull out assignments.

Have work contracts with reward as incentive.

Have pupils go to the board and write on it.

Gear seatwork to individual's ability.

Let friends work together on assignments.

Shorten concepts; break them into three or four parts.

Relate their experience stories to standard English.

Use the bizarre and unusual in teaching lesson (use magic in science, volcano working in class).

Have class write and tell why they enjoyed certain lesson.

Motivate through singing and dancing.

Pupils have option to have their work corrected or not.

Don't use grades; there is no failure.

Individualization; sometimes with a programmed learning packet and a reward system follow through.

Have before and after school projects and activities.

Develop black studies and other ethnic courses for whole school.

Teach to read phonetically so children can understand assignments.

Try to create curriculum areas that are not a part of elementary school program.

Have many actitivies going on in room.

Have a wood shop in room to teach measurement.

5. Teacher's materials:

Puppets, animals, toys.

Newspaper articles.

Magazines.

Teacher-made materials to go along with basal reader and mathematics text.

Musical instruments.

Poems.

Visual aids (filmstrips, slides, overhead transparencies).

Reading series, Miami linguistics that has puppets to go along with stories.

Puzzles, clay, sandpaper letters to help children figure out words.

Tape recorder for language reading development, other lessons.

Manipulative materials, teaching aids.

New textbooks in reading and mathematics.

Games.

Films.

Experience charts.

Records.

Pictures.

Comic books, books.

Find or make materials.

Stories.

Photographs of neighborhood and kids.

6. Teacher involves other teachers, community, administration:

    Ask other teachers for advice.

    Bring people into class to talk to kids.

    Bring in people who know more about subject than you do.

    Change teachers for more interest.

    Bring in own materials (game, musical instruments, educational aids) and share them with other teachers.

    Take kids to our homes.

PROBLEM: Pupils have difficulty thinking in abstract terms.

STRATEGIES:
1. Teacher involves other teachers, administration:

Talk to mathematics specialists about how to present abstract ideas.

Student teacher works with slower group or individually with children.

Ask other teachers for advice, outside reading sources.

2. Teacher involves community, agencies, parent groups:

Go on field trips.

Invite resource people to class.

Use specialists within the community.

3. Teacher's techniques:

Talk about movies and how different things are represented.

Have group discussions on how communication affects others and how it influences what happens to them.

Reads book way over their heads to interest them.

Relate abstract thinking to problem solving.

Don't make pupil feel babyish if he uses material objects.

Try to find motivation behind questions children ask.

Let them ask as many questions as they want.

Encourage verbalization, conversation in students.

Incorporate abstract ideas (sadness, happiness) in reading.

Speak on simple terms to begin with; break problems down.

Divide class into two groups: those who can think abstractly and those who cannot; work with them separately or individually.

Role play concerning abstract concept (e.g., prejudice).

Have children discover things for themselves (inquiry learning).

Child can work as long as he wants; no time periods.

Use analogies and give wide exposure to new words.

Go from concrete to abstract; invent ways so student becomes conscious of controlled imagination (e.g., look at leaf cells under microscope) then transfer this concrete knowledge to an abstract grasp of cells in other life forms, such as the human body.

Relate ideas in words from their environment and/or experience; be as concrete as possible; show simple and physical examples of an abstract concept.

Build visual images; use story problems (especially in mathematics); draw pictures.

Use fables, folklore, and fantasies; "imagine you are. . . ."

Use small group discussions and peer influence to increase interest.

Use all possible resources; e.g., experience charts, brought in pet, TV, drawings, building.

Body movement creativity uses—active involvement to integrate abstraction.

Make learning an active process; e.g., have kids dress up and put on plays about other countries or stories they have read.

Work on mathematics and reading skills.

Provide new experiences and have kids talk and write about them.

Use word problems in mathematics.

Work with students from where they are and take small learning steps.

Try to get students to look on me as person with something to offer; e.g., another way to think about things.

Talk about feelings, and then to self-concept.

4. Teacher's materials:

Use as many concrete materials as possible.

Give children manipulative materials to work with as long as they need them.

Play games, matching games.

Use films and pictures to show things they have not experienced.

Make up my own books on things outside of their environment.

Use pictures to clarify abstractions.

Use visual aids (sticks, cutouts, clay).

Provide newspaper, worksheets with analogies, colorful pictures, checkers, 3-D tic-tac-toe, soma blocks, library books.

Use current events that are relevant (to their experience), supplementary materials and exercises.

Bring in new materials to make own materials.

5. General statements:

Have certain abstract questions which pupils work on.

I ask questions and give assignments which require thought and discovery.

Constantly rehash and review.

PROBLEM: Pupils are frequently absent.

STRATEGIES:
1.   Teacher involves parent:

Techniques Reported For This Strategy

Demand absentee notes from parents.

Tell parents how children can make up work.

Phone parents—"what's the matter," "send kids to school," "can I help," etc.

Aide calls parents—"what's the matter," etc.

Home visits—encourage attendance to parents.

Parents participate, assume responsibility to reduce absences of child.

2.   Teacher involves student:

Show my concern; importance of school.

Send homework to absentees.

Have attendance awards.

Praise; encourage children to attend.

Make them want to be in class; make lessons/class more interesting; have continuous multiday activities, must be there first day to participate.

Inform class of next day's activities.

Ask child about absences/reasons for, etc.

Plan trips, extra class activities.

Deprive privileges for tardiness, unexcused absenteeism.

Students must do makeup work when they're absent.

Welcome them back, "missed you," etc.

Use a buddy system.

Give returning absentees more attention/time.

Set up doctor appointments to permit class attendance.

Have learning contracts which frequently absent students like and work to complete.

3. Teacher involves community, agencies, parent groups:

   If frequent absences, get help from agencies (e.g., child welfare, home visits, home/school coordinator, parent visitor).

   Don't call attendance officer, etc.

   Have close working relationship with county health center.

   At last resort, personal referral to social worker.

4. Teacher involves other teachers, aides, administration:

   Get help from administration, principal, guidance counselor.

   Get help from nurse if illness caused.

   Aide takes attendance.

   Contact school authorities or home/school coordinator who either visits homes or phones parents.

5. Teacher assumes responsibility:

   Get them clothes if that's the cause of absences.

PROBLEM: There is not enough time to plan the curriculum.

STRATEGIES:

1. Teacher meets curriculum demands through innovation or use of own time:

   Techniques Reported For This Strategy

   Take work in special subject groups.

   Special PTA meetings to meet parents in subject area.

   Let students do a lot of their own planning.

   Have students do some of their own grading.

   Use aide in classroom when appropriate, as proctors and moderators.

   Have made individualized programs.

   Plan curriculum in advance (a year, etc.).

   Have group planning meetings at teacher's home.

   Use planning guides.

   Cut out repetition in curriculum.

   Make time for planning.

   Do some planning in transit to and from school.

   Take work home.

   Use free time at school (breaks, lunches, etc.).

   Use weekends.

   Do it in class while working on something else.

   Do before and after school.

   Use summer vacation time.

Take other teachers' classes to give them planning times.

Teachers share materials and ideas for curriculum.

Ask for specialists' help.

Coordinate planning time with other teachers.

2. Teachers use release time:

Administration provides planning periods.

Use release time.

3. General statements:

Attend workshops.

Plan on more work at beginning of year.

Complain a lot to policymakers regarding lack of planning time during school day.

Try to get intragrade level meetings.

Try to get meetings with teachers to coordinate grade level needs and goals.

PROBLEM: There is a large percentage of pupil turnover.

STRATEGIES:
1. Teacher integrates new students into class:

Techniques Reported For This Strategy

Give extra attention: talk to, listen, show interest.

Set up individualized goals for new child.

Sometimes rely on other teachers for grouping advice.

Tutor new child for awhile.

Assess new student myself.

Use a buddy system to establish friendship ties.

Make new child feel welcome; introduce him to class/routine.

Accept situation despite annoyance.

Look at new student's report card/records, place him.

Brainstorming: talk to former teachers if possible about their observations.

Establish special group for new students.

Aide should assist new child too.

Re-form study groups.

2.   Teacher and departing student:

Have party for student.

Ask principal if student could stay at school.

Send report on child to new teacher.

3.   Other strategies:

Help parents of new student.

Invite parents of new child to school.

Choose my own pupils.

PROBLEM: Pupils have language difficulties.

STRATEGIES:
1.   Teacher involves parents:

Techniques Reported For This Strategy

Told my aide (mother of child in class) not to speak Spanish at home.

Try to get parents to help Spanish-speaking child.

Speak Spanish with parents.

Parent conferences.

2. Teacher involves student, student assumes some responsibility:

    Use peer tutoring and peer interpreting (bilingual with new students).

    Have group discussions in reading; group interaction for learning English.

    Child can choose from file box of worksheets in language arts.

    Role playing or dramatization using English and Spanish.

3. Teacher's personal approach:

    Tell them not to cuss too loud because I don't know any bad words.

    Encourage pride in Spanish language.

    Correct mildly so child is reassured.

    I'm very exaggerated and animated.

    Am patient with them; don't let it bother me; accept their language.

    Don't say anything about having difficulties in front of class.

4. Teacher's techniques:

    Encourage them to read as much as possible.

    Use music, plays, and poetry.

Take field trips.

Stress word endings.

Talk to them alot; get them to talk while working; have them practice talking softly.

Try to get them to use complete sentences.

Find non-English student's interests in his language.

Work individually with children on language problems.

Use pictures; they say it in Spanish, I say it in English.

Have lots of oral reports and discussions.

Take to library once a week to check out books.

Have language arts programs.

Repetition of poems, songs, and choral reading.

Drills on sounds of words, phonics.

Use math to help with grammar.

Stress grammar.

Use any training in ESL*.

Use the languages (e.g., Chinese, English, Spanish, street English) that the student uses at home in class; make kids bi- or trilingual; encourage participating regardless of language.

Stress writing essays and other writing.

Tape speech, then play back for pronunciation exercises.

Stress memorization of new language.

---

*ESL: See page 33.

First get definitions of words down.

Let them use dictionary to find word definitions.

Use "my favorite word" technique to learn words.

Use Spanish in some class lessons; teach Spanish to whole class.

Speak native language to student who is new; use the slang words in class; use dialect to explain words.

Correct their language or pronunciation; use myself as an example; ask them to concentrate on saying words correctly.

Speak clearly and make certain they understand directions.

Tell them there are several different English languages in the United States and that home language may be different from standard.

Stress standard English.

5. Teacher's materials:

Use Peabody language kit, tape recorder, Fernald writing techniques, Hilt materials, Behavior Research Labs materials, R. Lados techniques.

Use ESL materials.

Use flash cards; pictures for word associations.

Games emphasizing standard English.

Visual aids, filmstrips; have students draw story the next day.

Make own materials; buy supplementary materials, manipulation materials.

6. Teacher involves other teachers or aides:

Have special classes for those pupils newly arrived in country (non-English speaking).

Bilingual teacher works with them twice a week or part of the day; ESL Tutoring program; special aides or special teachers.

Volunteer reading program people help students.

Rely on translation by aides.

Got ideas on teaching skills from language teacher.

Refer those with hearing problems to nurse.

7. Other strategies:

Take special reading classes.

PROBLEM: Pupils often achieve below grade norm.

STRATEGIES:
1. Teacher involves parents:

    Techniques Reported For This Strategy

    Send work home so parents can help; send letter to parents for their help.

    Parents sign learning contracts.

2. Teacher involves student, student assumes some responsibility:

    Self-evaluation by pupils.

    Cross-age, peer, and sibling tutoring.

    Let students run errands.

3. Teacher's personal approach:

    Don't force them to do work.

    Raise my expectations within reasonable means.

Show them their achievements; build their self-confidence; priase them when they do well.

Push them a little more than the others.

Don't tell them they are below grade level.

Make them understand they can achieve and that they do as well as anyone else.

We (teachers) are very demanding and expect them to attain goals.

Don't publicize what the gap is; eliminate stigma.

Don't yell at them or be mean.

4. Teacher's techniques:

Explain how to do tests; introduce materials to be used on tests.

Tell why learning is important; what their level is and what it should be.

Work in small groups.

Test them at beginning of year for placement.

Use child's interest to bring about achievement.

Use ability groupings.

Give special help to slower children (during snack time).

Give slow ones extra seatwork and time at special centers.

Let quicker children work on their own.

Work with slow group first.

Give them more time to master concepts.

Drill on reading skills.

Work individually with children as much as possible.

Go over and over material until they master it—repetition and reinforcement.

Stress library use.

Request special education.

Have afterschool activities.

Teach them to think things out on their own.

Make structured homework assignments.

Keep assignments on file.

Have class reading club.

Encourage creative writing.

Have double reading/math periods as necessary.

Set an example; speak correctly.

Motivate by prizes, rewards.

5. Teacher's curriculum:

Individualize work; design program from their present level that can bring them up in increments to what they need to know.

Stress math and reading skills with time available in this curriculum.

Teach them what they will be tested on—SRA materials.

Use provided curriculum.

6. Teacher's materials:

Cut and paste assignments.

Enrichment activities from basal readers.

Multisensory program: pictures, charts, stories, cassettes, headphones, viewers, records, films.

Use films and records to help improve reading skills.

Games and manipulative materials.

Dolch reading 220-word list.

Use high interest, relevant, concrete subject materials.

Buy materials on my own for class/supplementary.

7. Teacher involves other teachers, administrators:

Enlist aid of others (psychologist, aide, other teachers, principal, specialists, librarian, volunteer tutor); field trips.

8. Other strategies:

Tell children to work to the best of their ability; make them work as hard as possible; put your foot down and make them learn; take it as it comes; teach basic skills based on tests taken.

PROBLEM: Unattended physical problems such as poor eyesight and deafness impede pupils' learning.

STRATEGIES:
1. Teacher involves parent:

Techniques Reported For This Strategy

Ask parents if child is on medication.

Communicate situation to parents by phone/notes/visits.

Participate with parents to see action taken.

2. Teacher involves student:

Place poor eyesight, hearing kids to front of room.

Ask kids to do what they can.

Observe children's responses in classroom.

Use more mimeographs instead of chalkboard.

Ask child if anything is wrong with him.

3. Teacher involves community, agencies, and/or parent groups:

PTA sometimes pays if parent can't.

Find out about free services for child (for parent too).

Notify local agencies, home/school coordinator, social worker.

4. Teacher involves other teachers, administration:

Checks through school nurse, medical personnel.

No school nurse, I take care of minor injuries/check-ups.

School tests eyes, ears, teeth, gives shots.

Refer student to guidance office/counselor/principal/administration.

Send them to health clinic.

Nurse contacts parents.

5. Other strategies:

Use free glasses, medical and dental care made possible by donations and federal programs.

Teacher takes child/parents to health clinic.

Parent coordinator takes child and parent to health appointment.

6. General statements:

Live with the problem.

Check their cumulative health record.

PROBLEM: Pupils have little confidence in their ability to achieve.

STRATEGIES:
1. Teacher involves parents:

Techniques Reported For This Strategy

Encourage parents to come to class; bring parents in as resource people, boost pupils' ego.

Contact with parents: notes home, ask for support for me and children; talk to parents and tell them to make sure students do homework (older brothers and sisters, too).

Send notes home if child did exceptionally well that day; ask parent to praise child.

2. Teacher involves student, student assumes some responsibility:

Ask child what he likes to do.

Get students' excited about receiving perfect paper.

Cross-age or cross-ability tutoring (younger children are tutored by child).

Give child management position for project.

Help them to develop peer group bond to lift each other.

3. Teacher discusses, explains:

Discussion with individual child on abilities, say that progress is its own reward; discuss in general discussion, using example forms.

4. Teacher tells student:

   Tell child to do it on their own; tell kids what my minimum expectations and rules are; tell them some of the work is so hard they can't do it; tell them they can do better; tell them to do their best; tell them they'll get cheated someday if they don't learn certain things.

5. Teacher's personal approach:

   Teacher's statements about child's capacities to child: tell kids they are just as gifted as anyone; state that he can do something. I believe in the children and my confidence in them helps them to believe in themselves; always compliment whether work is good or bad; have or set high expectations; believe every child can do something; tell children if one is slow in math, he may perform well in another subject; tell children they don't have to be like everybody else. Boys enjoy being called "gentlemen and scholars," tell them how important they are; tell girls that being a girl isn't a handicap.

   Teachers encourage: examples are—give lots of encouragement, praise, and attention; encourage in areas where they are not doing well; build positive image by using constant positive verbal reinforcement; compliment them when they look nice and they continue to do so; pick leader to do something; motivate others to try.

   Teachers use of positive reinforcement: praise them when they succeed; reward child for accomplishments (letting him play with blocks by himself); give stars, say "that's right," holding up paper in class; making a big deal out of progress; artificially continue situations that give him success; "monkey business" game—working kids get pay which lets them buy things in class (trips, popcorn). Positive form of reference, display papers, give badges for good work, charts that show progress, sign that says, "I can."

   Give kids things to do that give them a feeling of achievement: making things, doing errands, having duties, "responsibilities," even if they can't read; start with things they can do; start work for them sometimes; call on kids when I think they know the answer or have something to say that they want the class to hear; build up self-image.

Play down any failure the child has; when student is frustrated, leave them alone; try not to criticize; ignore some behavior; ask them to ask me to help them when they need me.

Don't over-expect at the beginning of the year; recognize them as individuals (ask them about their family—mother, father); physically give them a pat on the back; ask the child why he hasn't achieved; tell them race is not a problem; stress what learning can do for them; take a warm-up time each day to see where they are emotionally; if hyperactive, let him go out into the hall; keep them not too close to kids who are successful; make children realize they are more important than their grades.

6. Teacher's techniques:

Individualized attention: afterschool attention; give students work they can succeed at and then bring them up in increments of success; work with students individually and on individual assignments; get them to the board and show them how to do it; when a child brings something in, we use it as a kickoff for a new lesson or study.

Grouping: low achieving group is worked with independently away from rest of class; let kids work in. Always have a review before a test; keep diary on kids' behavior; use them to point out good behavior changes; give clear simple directions; discussions and writing exercises on "things I can do" at beginning of year; have child look at this when frustrated throughout the year; use self-corrective materials; posters across doorways regarding success; have kids write "help" on papers when they need it; give very few tests; use games for reading, bulletin boards with manipulative materials, use films, tape recordings.

7. Teacher's curriculum and grades:

Open structure curriculum; make it interesting; let them work with whom they like; many innovative things; team teaching;

open space curriculum; bought books on their level; use basic academics.

Grades: don't grade anyone below a C, have conference reports. No report cards: individualize grading (not on a 100% system); have an ungraded situation; always chance to make up a sad face for a happy face; use conference reports rather than report cards.

Put comments rather than marks on papers; write "superfine" on papers the slow kids have done well.

8. Teacher involves community:

    Call volunteer agencies to help children.

9. Teacher involves other teachers, principal, administration:

    Send SOS to other teachers who come to room unannounced and praise students; send child who has done well in another room to display his work where another teacher can praise the child; or grade it with an "A," hang up children's work; call volunteer agencies to help children.

    Pressure administration with formalizing some special classes.

    Use Glasser approach, *Schools Without Failure.*

10. Other strategies:

    Make kids aware of need for junior high; show need, point out that this last chance, stress importance of achieving.

    Don't look at their record.

    Discuss backgrounds of average and famous minority and non-minority group people.

11. General statements:

    Try to make things interesting; build up their ability level; let them experience success; try to push them; try to make things as real as possible.

Individuals tend to perceive the world based on their experiences in the process of living. When problems arise, they draw from those learned experiences and develop behaviors for coping with them. Sometimes they utilize appropriate strategies for solving a given problem and at times they do not.

The classroom teacher is no different from the larger society. Thus, we note that the problems and strategies from the teachers in this study represent a broad base attempt to deal with the real world issues facing them. Some of their perceptions about the child grow out of assumptions mentioned earlier in the chapter concerning the fact that professionals often perceive the inner city child as deficient educationally and socially. Other views from the teachers reflect an attempt to relate their instructional problems and the child's learning difficulties to the limitations in the school curriculum and related educational services.

The problem areas identified are clearly meaningful for the teachers in this study, and many of their strategies provide a framework for other professionals in the field. The challenge to the profession of teaching, however, is to be bold enough to insist that the school provide the necessary tools for teaching the inner city child. At the same time, the teachers need to be humane and creative enough to develop an instructional program based on the assumption that the inner city child can learn if properly taught in a supportive environment.

80

CHAPTER IV

COLLEAGUES AND SCHOOL STAFF PROBLEMS

The point has been made in previous sections that inner-city schools offer a magnitude of special problems for the professional staff. The support staff of the school also find themselves facing a number of unique problems which call for the combined efforts of professional and nonteaching personnel to work cooperatively together in order to maintain a quality program.

The need for a cooperative effort on the part of the school personnel is so important because there are students in our urban schools who are academically uninspired, some need health care, many are from impoverished homes, and there are a variety of other factors which are well calculated to increase the pressure on the total school staff. In addition, many of the schools are located in sections of the city where the poverty and other societal factors can add to an already depressive situation.

There is clear evidence that one of the central keys in developing a cooperative school environment rest with the leadership style of the instructional leader, the principal. Staff development program, in-service programs and communication between faculty and administrators play an especially effective role in building a cooperative atmosphere in the school, and minimizing some of the problems identified in colleague and school staff issues suggested by the teachers in this study. Teachers in successful school programs seem to have more opportunity for interchange of ideas and more time for joint planning, as well as establishing networks for utilization of paraprofessionals, volunteering parents and new staff members. This interaction provides an excellent model for opening the lines of communication and fostering a more cooperative spirit among *all* staff members in a school setting.

The teacher whose views were sought in this study had a variety of student, curricular, parental concerns and related colleague and staff problems. A list of the teacher problems are as follows:

1. Teachers resist new ideas.

2. There is low morale on this faculty.

3. Teachers have low expectations for pupil performance.

4. Teachers are afraid of pupils.

5. Custodians are uncooperative.

6. Teachers lack adequate preparation to teach in this school.

7. Teachers are prejudiced against pupils and parents.

8. More experienced teachers are not supportive to new teachers.

It is not unusual for inner-city teachers to feel a special press from many aspects in the school and community environment. A review of the strategies these teachers utilized to handle the problems they faced will offer some guidance for those of us working in the field.

PROBLEM: Teachers resist new ideas.

STRATEGIES:
1. Teacher directs or advises other teachers:

   Techniques Reported For This Strategy

   Talk to them patiently like to my students.

   Praise them for ideas.

   Bring up my own innovative ideas to other teachers.

   Ask for help in planning new programs.

   Advise teachers to make home visits.

2. Teacher involves other teachers actively:

   Work closely with teachers on my grade level, team.

   Invite other teachers into my room and vice versa.

   Use peer pressure among teachers.

   Show other teachers what I'm doing; share, etc.

   Organize social events for teachers.

   Try ideas of other teachers.

   Participate in workshops, inservice classes.

3. Other strategies:

   Tell students in my own class to talk to other students about new ideas.

   Get help from administration if resistance is hindering students.

   Get parents on your side.

Respect other teachers' ideas.

Don't force others to accept my ideas.

May use faculty-rejected ideas in my class if it works.

4. General statements:

Avoid or ignore the problem.

Do what I think is right.

Set an example.

PROBLEM: There is low morale on this faculty.

STRATEGIES:
1. Teacher directs or advises other teachers:

   Techniques Reported For This Strategy

   Try to help teachers understand minority children.

   Speak frankly and hope that you can gain other teachers' confidence.

   Talk to other teachers on the team.

   Build other teachers' confidence.

   Remain cheerful; it rubs off on other teachers.

2. Teacher actively involves other teachers:

   Talks about problems in informal meetings and/or inservice meetings.

   Exchange teaching techniques with younger teachers.

   Share high morale with other high morale teachers.

   Have meetings with team leader once a week.

Have faculty parties and special events; teacher clubs.

Observe other classes and vice versa.

Lend an open ear and closed mouth.

Help other teachers when asked and vice versa.

Try to work effectively with other teachers.

Take other teachers on home visits with me.

Talk of future plans to other teachers.

3. Other strategies:

Get help from principal.

Sit down and talk about problems with students.

Plan activities for the community.

4. General statements:

Do the best I can with what I have.

Rely on my personality.

Try to bolster faculty morale.

PROBLEM: Teachers have low expectations for pupil perfromance.

STRATEGIES:
1. Teacher tries to influence other teachers:

Techniques Reported For This Strategy

Suggest new ways to teach child.

Tell teachers that children can sense lack of respect teachers have toward them.

85

Discuss why they feel they have low expectations, they don't expect much because of child's background.

Advocates individualized instruction.

Talk out the problem with the teacher.

Encourage self-examination of other teachers regarding interest/attitude.

Talk to other teachers and tell them a child needs special help and can succeed.

Show off my kinds of work to other teachers.

Let other teachers into my room to see what I'm doing.

Discuss ideas in nonthreatening way.

2. Teacher's personal approach:

Have high expectations and standards; children respond.

Treat pupils with respect.

Believe all children can learn.

Ignore the fallacy that teachers have low expectations for pupils.

3. Teacher's interaction with students:

Say positive things to the students (nothing negative).

Work individually with child.

Show students that all teachers aren't alike.

Use children's energies in constructive way.

Try to help students understand why they have to do what they have to do.

Give lessons to class on various community helpers.

Capitalize on peer pressure.

Praise children when they try to accomplish anything.

Show kids where to get information; act as resource person.

Try to establish high pupil self-esteem, good feelings, positive attitude about themselves and classmates.

Don't give many grades.

Make material more interesting, challenging.

Reward children when they accomplish something.

Change curriculum for children's success.

Use ability groupings—students learn from their peers.

Exchange students with other classes.

Judge children on basis of work not previous teacher's evaluations.

Motivate child by letting him see what future could be if he performs.

4. Teacher interaction with other teachers, administration:

Discuss innovations at faculty meetings.

Have group discussions.

Principal had teachers set goals individually per student.

5. Other strategies:

Note capabilities of child for next teacher.

Tell class they are low groups.

Set up own classroom rules—follow them.

6. General statements:

Use principal; he helps alot.

PROBLEM: Teachers are afraid of pupils.

STRATEGIES:
1. Teacher tries to help other teachers who are afraid:

Techniques Reported For This Strategy

Show teachers pupils are just human beings not to be feared.

Tell teachers to see assitant principal for help.

Tell other teachers that if they continue to be afraid they won't get anything done.

Discuss conduct, problems and fears.

Invite new teachers into classroom.

Give suggestions; tell other teachers to talk to children on their level; talk it out with them.

Talk to child individually; respect one another.

Tell other teacher my perceptions of fear situation.

2. Teacher's techniques:

Ask help from other teachers concerning student problems.

Get your bluff in; don't let him know he or she scares you; come on strong at beginning of the school year.

Make home visits.

Call or write parents about discipline.

Take pupils out to shop, movies, sports events.

Become friendly with child but still discipline him.

Involve students in learning activity.

Talk problems out with student.

Encourage students to come in and visit.

Let students know where you stand and what you stand for.

3. General statements:

Can't do much about other teachers.

Helped by a good sense of humor.

Overcome this through experience.

If they don't see you as a threat, you won't see them as a threat.

PROBLEM: Custodians are uncooperative.

STRATEGIES:

1. Teacher's personal approach:

Techniques Reported For This Strategy

Be very friendly with custodian.

Once you know them, there is no problem with repairs.

Treat them as people.

Ask for help when needed.

Keep after him.

Go to head custodian.

89

Have suggestion box for him.

Give head custodian Christmas present.

Include them as part of faculty luncheons.

2.   Teachers seek help:

Go to principal, assistant principal.

Notify parents of situation at school.

3.   Teacher assumes responsibility:

Keep room clean with help from kids.

Do it myself.

Help him with my own room cleanup.

Bring in supplies myself.

PROBLEM: Teachers lack adequate preparation to teach in this school.

STRATEGIES:
1.   Teacher involves other teachers, administration:

Techniques Reported For This Strategy

Help other teachers set up classroom.

Ask other teachers for help and advice.

Prepare good classes; set an example.

Share materials with other teachers.

Acquaint new teachers with community; relate own inner-city background to middle class teachers.

Ask help from principal; talk to administration.

Discuss and compare with teachers the pupils' backgrounds.

Team teach according to ability levels.

Encourage other teachers.

Attend grade level meetings; workshops.

Demonstrate in my class for unprepared teachers.

Share my ideas with other teachers; make suggestions.

2. Teacher concerned with future teachers:

Talk to professors about changing curriculums to meet inner-city needs.

Talk up my program with college students.

3. Other strategies:

Take courses; do outside reading (library, etc.).

Visit parents for better understanding of children.

Take inservice training program while teaching.

Learn by teaching.

PROBLEM: Teachers are prejudiced against pupils and parents.

STRATEGIES:
1. Teacher involves parents:

Techniques Reported For This Strategy

Talk to parents; phone them at home.

Try to involve parents in class.

Visit child's home.

Ignore hostility of parent; rather handle parents with understanding as people.

2. Teacher involves student:

Use reading games which discuss prejudice.

Treat and think about child positively.

Role play; let kids play teacher role.

Take field trips.

Ignore student hostility; rather praise child when appropriate for good work, appropriate behavior, etc.

3. Teacher involves other teachers, administration, community:

Set an example.

Try to change attitudes; talk to them; set an example.

Try to get teachers to emphathize with parents and children in urban school setting.

Speak up at faculty meetings, lounge, lunch.

Don't listen to what other teachers say.

Have workshops; small group discussions.

Don't discuss children with other children.

Listen alot, but don't say much.

Get help from principal or administrator; organize group discussions.

4. Other strategies:

When there is a teacher/student personality conflict, I put student in my room until teacher has calmed down.

Evaluate my personal feelings about students and their life-style.

PROBLEM: More experienced teachers are not supportive to new teachers.

STRATEGIES:
1.   Teacher involves other teachers:

Techniques Reported For This Strategy

Meet other teachers socially.

Ask them for advice/aid.

Visit other classrooms and vice versa.

Work with other teachers on attitudes.

Share ideas, volunteer services.

Let other teachers know of my problems.

Share materials with them.

Praise other teachers.

2.   Teacher involves administration:

Buddies assigned to new teachers.

Grade level meetings to discuss ideas.

Talk to principal about helping new teachers to adjust within the inner-city school setting.

3.   Other strategies:

Seek help from college professors.

Do outside reading.

Discuss at faculty meetings.

Help from teacher trainer.

4. General statements:

Support other new teachers.

Do what I think is right.

Try not to impose my ideas on them.

Respect their ideas, treat them as human beings.

Act as mediator.

The pressures faced by the teaching staff and nonteaching personnel in the inner-city school are real. It is easy for school personnel to attempt to reduce some of their own sense of frustration by finding fault with a colleague. When the fault-finding becomes a common occurrence, teacher performance suffers and the general morale in the school is low.

It is against this backdrop of low morale problems that such charges as poor preparation on the part of teachers and racial and social class insensitivity are likely to emerge. Such is the picture of professional unrest that is highlighted in this chapter on colleague and staff problems.

The principal and other key personnel have a special role to play in clearing the air so that both the teaching and nonteaching personnel can work effectively together. In addition, the principal must be sensitive to the manner in which the teachers interact with all children in the school regardless of social class and ethnicity.

Teachers also have a responsibility to maintain a fair and honest posture toward each person in the school, whether they are professional or nonprofessional. Equally important, teachers must maintain a climate of support for the school program so that the children can sense that they care for them and perceive the school as a worthwhile place for teachers to teach and children to learn.

CHAPTER V

SCHOOL ADMINISTRATION PROBLEMS

The chief administrator of an inner-city school is the major force behind creating a climate for productive programmatic change and for creating a high level of morale. Urban schools are often plagued with a high teacher turnover, teachers who have limited preparation for teaching in that type of situation, community pressures and problems which spill over into the school, and inadequate budgets for enriching the curriculum. With all of these problems and issues, the principal must develop strategies designed to increase the effectiveness of the teachers, to build a strong instructional program, and to maintain appropriate opportunities for community groups to provide input into the school.

Administration is an activity concerned with the smooth operation of the school. It is, as suggested by Robert Owens (1970), "the processes which help the organization operate its mechanisms for achieving its goals." The principal who is the administrative leader within the school is then the facilitator of the processes. The principal clarifies the goals of the school and works with various members of the staff and community in achieving these goals.

A major ingredient for any successful school is the maintenance of a high level of morale among the teachers. James Curtin (1964) noted that "high morale is characterized by a number of conditions, but among these perhaps the most important for fulfilling the purposes of supervision are confidence, security, ambition, and zeal for self improvement. Where one finds these, one finds morale of a higher order."

The type of behavior and leadership a supervising administrator exhibits are, to a great extent, what determines success. Administrative behavior that is typified by attitudes of acceptance and support appear to have a positive effect on morale. The enhancement of morale, in turn, tends to increase the power of the school to hold its staff and to generate a feeling that each teacher is important to the work of the school. Some of the problem areas identified are as follows:

1. Administration is not responsive to community and parents.

2. Administration is unresponsive to the instructional needs of the teachers.

3. The school board is not representative of the community and is not responsive to it.

4. Administration provides insufficient support for discipline problems.

5. Administration does not provide adequate leadership for innovation.

6. Teachers have to spend too much time on recordkeeping and other paperwork.

These problems reflect the major concerns of the group of teachers involved in this study. The strategies that they utilized to solve these problems can be evaluated in terms of their experience and perceptions as professionals in the field.

PROBLEM: Administration is not responsive to community and parents.

STRATEGIES:
1.   Teacher involves parents:

Techniques Reported For This Strategy

Get parents' ideas and do best I can; send home question-naire.

Give parents books and old classroom texts or books about what goes on in school.

Discuss available programs; discipline in home.

Parents go to board, newspapers and demonstrate if they don't get cooperation.

Deal with parents as a teacher and not as part of adminis-tration.

Contact parents: phone, talk, write, introduce self, give pro-gress reports; visit parents.

Invite parents to come in and observe class; discuss mutual goals.

Parent-teacher conferences.

Ask parents without children at home to come in and help.

Parents voluntarily work at school.

Meet parents when they bring children to my home; let them see where I live.

2.   Teacher involves students:

Organize a basketball team and coach it (really gets parents involved).

Encourage students to invite parents to class and PTA.

Encourage students to take work home for parents to see how they stand with rest of class.

Children sold candy to raise money; teacher helped.

3. Teacher involves community, agencies, parent groups:

Tell principal what I learned from talking to parents.

Attend community meetings: talk to parents and get them on our side.

Title I requires administration to include parents in planning.

4. Teacher involves other teachers, administration:

Don't get involved in political arrangements.

Told administration and teachers I'd worked with parents and arranged for tutor so they'd see it is possible to work with parents.

Suggested to principal that he hire minorities.

Publicity from my ecology program stirred administration.

Group of teachers united and tried to go around the administration.

Assistant principal deals with principal who has no respect for parents.

5. Other strategies:

Have parties for whole family.

Relate better to parents as a coach than as a teacher.

Children come to my home to work around it; parties.

Plan events where both school personnel and community get together even on a social basis.

Speak up for what I think is right—as in telling parents of two fighting boys which child was right (administration dislikes this).

PROBLEM: Administration is unresponsive to the instructional needs of the teachers.

STRATEGIES:
1. Teacher involves students to compensate for administration:

    Techniques Reported For This Strategy

    Kids help write books, make materials, competitive games.

    Kids film school activities to show other kids.

2. Teacher involves other teachers, administrators:

    Go to assistant principal and avoid principal; former is more cooperative.

    Meet with school board and faculty.

    Write to the board each year.

    Express indignation over misuse or waste of materials.

    Convince principal I need administrative support.

    Use responsive teachers for advice, share materials, share ability.

    Inform administrator of other materials and ideas; suggest inservice training.

    Invite administrator to class to see problems.

    Ask secretaries what to do or who to see.

    Hash out needs at teacher's meetings.

    Talk to people from urban Teacher Corps.

100

Keep administrator informed of how we intend to use materials.

Ask for a meeting between teachers and principals to make it a group project.

Suggest ways community people can be contacted for certain supplies.

Get faculty on my side when I present list of demands.

Present program to administrator and seek funds.

Go to resource people: grade chairman, consultant.

I gripe alot to administration; pressure it.

3.   Teacher involves parents, community:

Parents, teachers, and children sold candy and showed movies to raiše money for materials.

Talk to parents and inform them of lack of materials.

PTA helps; community helps us with money and materials.

4.   Teacher assumes responsibility:

Buy things myself.

Bring in things myself (e.g., films from library).

Make my own things; go to the junkyard.

Try to get it; find out when stockroom will be refilled.

Improvise and use own resources.

Do all work from mimeo and chalkboard; not enough books.

Use games the Teacher Corps gave us in training.

Do with what I have and use if effectively.

Present experiment in different way if unable to get proper equipment (e.g., go to cafeteria when unable to get hot plate to study steam).

Get things from other schools or teachers at other schools.

5.   Other strategies:

Keep up on current educational methods; take classes; active in reading associations and committees.

Attend useful outside conferences and conventions, workshops.

Make field trips so kids can see things they are learning about.

Read books for ideas.

Have to spend all money ahead of time because principal spends half of it for his needs.

PROBLEM: The school board is not representative of the community and is not responsive to it.

STRATEGIES:
1.   Teacher involves parents, community:

Techniques Reported For This Strategy

Talk with county paraprofessionals.

Take problems to community.

Talk to a school board member.

Inform parents of school board's activities.

Belong to community groups.

Have socials and meetings for parents at school.

Encourage people to indicate county concern.

Make home visits.

Call or notify parent about school and class activities.

2. Teacher involves other teachers, administration:

Talk to principal.

Talk to other teachers about it.

Talk to consultant.

Attend school board meetings.

PROBLEM: Administration provides insufficient support for discipline problems.

STRATEGIES:
1. Teacher involves parents:

Techniques Reported For This Strategy

Send note to parent.

Speak to/call parents.

Conferences with parent.

Parent/teacher takes child home.

Child cannot return until parent comes to school for conference.

Ask parent to support me; make follow-up calls and place memo in child's accumulative folder.

2. Teacher involves student:

Have group discussion regarding discipline and authority.

Give problem children responsibility.

Help from kids; one or two help control situation.

Role play discipline situation; pupil assumes role of teacher dealing with problem students; use upper grade children in programs; modeling.

Have many activities for pupils; keep them interested and contained in class.

Let kids have voice in organization of room.

Write essay, "Why I misbehaved."

Punish: isolate, take away free time, lunch, play time, privileges, do exercises (exercise through recess), stay after school.

Take child out of room to rap and give others seatwork to do while I'm gone.

Reward good student behavior.

3.   Teacher involves other teachers, administration:

Exchange kids among ourselves and with different teams.

Discuss problems with principal and vice principal.

Work with administration aide.

Principal/parent/teacher conference.

Consult principal when necessary.

Refer to school psychologist or social worker, guidance counselor.

Tell staff trainer and principal when I dislike the approach of the school psychologist.

4.   Other strategies; do not involve administration:

Handle problems myself.

Use the self-discipline table.

Tell them to take walk and give them hall pass.

Started "respect yourself" campaign (played record) and made kids aware of behavior.

Don't use corporal punishment.

Avoid a confrontation I think I might not be able to handle in my room.

Use point system: kids earn points and get fruit or sugarless candy.

Manipulate environment or child's response to it to eliminate problem causing discipline problems (e.g., work with smaller learning blocks to learn a concept).

Show disapproval with a frown.

Go to director of inservice program for help.

5. General statements:

If you can't handle your own kids, you shouldn't teach.

Discipline should be firm, fair, and consistent.

Don't have discipline problems because I'm strict.

Ignore it unless I'm affected.

Try to change attitude of at least one of the two who can't get along.

PROBLEM: Administration does not provide adequate leadership for innovation.

STRATEGIES:
1. Teachers innovate without administration's leadership:

Techniques Reported For This Strategy

Innovate in my own room: new ideas, materials, willing to experiment, be my own leader, lay job on the line.

Set up cross-age tutoring with other classes.

Ignore lack of leadership.

Let kids do what they want.

Can do what I want in my self-contained classroom.

Other teachers share ideas, even from other schools.

Getting teachers to share is an innovation in itself.

Let others see what works; their attitudes change.

Present new ideas to administration and other teachers; discuss jointly, explain, convince, tell them how I feel about them.

Ask if they'll let me do my ideas; if not, I don't bug them.

Request visiting rights to other classes and bring back whatever is of value.

Bring in and share new materials at faculty meetings.

Use ideas learned at workshops.

2. Teachers innovate with some administrative approval:

Get help from consultants.

Try to convince principal and consultant to push harder for something to be provided.

Request workshops for new ideas.

Use teacher-trainee's ideas.

Some curricular programs helpful; multisensory programs, corrective reading.

If what I do is not liked, we discuss it.

Find out those in administration who do provide leadership.

3. Teachers innovate against administration's disapproval:

    Teachers united and rebelled against principal and with our pooled ideas we don't need principal's help.

    Tell principal what I want her to know.

4. Other strategies:

    Am working successfully without basal readers.

    Take graduate courses to learn new methods.

    Innovate through experience, periodicals, media, education, and journal articles.

    Get help from creative friends.

PROBLEM: Teachers have to spend too much time on recordkeeping and other paperwork.

STRATEGIES:
1. Teacher adapts to meet paperwork demands:

    Techniques Reported For This Strategy

    Take it home—do outside of class; before or after school.

    Use preparation period.

    Start paperwork ahead of time.

    Keep up—do it as it comes in.

Make carbons of everything (charts with their names).

Holidays and weekends, semester breaks, inservice days.

Use lunch period, breakfast, between classes.

I have it down to a system; can finish in prep period or breakfast.

I do it but am chronically late; ignore until last minute.

Make up codes and other simple ways to keep records.

Make mental notes and write it at another time.

I make the time—just do it.

Take time out from class; give children busy work.

Promise kids if they're quiet while I do it we'll go outside.

2.   Teacher seeks alternatives:

Don't do charts that are worthless (dental charts, etc., just write down for those who do bring them in).

Cut it down to bare minimum; do what's important.

Eliminated daily rating—do it weekly or at end of project.

Don't keep or give grades, but have conferences.

Don't correct each work, just put general comment on paper.

Don't spend much time as it's not important.

Keep my comments simple.

3.   Teacher seeks help:

Share ideas with teachers on how to save time.

Help each other mimeograph.

Aide helps me; volunteers.

Students help: do lunch count; mark own papers (as teaching tool, use recordkeeping).

Have clerical help half days in June to catch up.

Share with team teachers.

Friends help me.

Have older children help me (play secretary); kids take attendance.

Give children work they can do without much instruction; this way they don't have to take much work home.

4. General statements:

Complain to parents; makes me feel better.

Keep track of progress from skill to skill.

Complain about amount of recordkeeping required to administration and seek alternative methods where appropriate.

The administrator's problems in the inner-city school are real and they call for "hands-on" decision making. The solutions must utilize all available resources—teachers, colleges, children, and the community. As the problems develop and prior to their development, the principal must work with the instructional staff, encouraging them to function within the school planning units to bring about change in methods and procedures. While operating as an instructional leader, the teachers with or without problems must be brought to realize that the leadership role, while humane and democratic, must also maintain a degree of autonomy in order to evaluate and coordinate the cooperative decision making.

Thus, the role of the urban administrator can be a unique position especially as it relates to the instructional and people problems of the school. Not only do they (urban administrators) have the problems that all administrators have, but their problems are compounded by the complexities of a student population with special needs. If, however, principals can quickly realize the nature of their special challenge, they can mobilize the staff to meet them. As they use all of their skills and abilities — technical, human, and conceptual — they can so guide the instructional program that the optimum of achievement is experienced by all students.

SUPPLIES

KAM

111

CHAPTER VI

SCHOOL RESOURCE PROBLEMS

Education in the United States is big business when it is seen in the light of appropriating the funds necessary to operate our vast educational enterprise. Our public school systems in the United States enroll millions of students from kindergartento grade 12 and spend billions of dollars in the process. In fact, as we look at education today, it is not unusual to note that public education has more people involved on a fulltime basis in its activities than any other segment of American life.

During the early stages of the "War on Poverty," some special efforts were developed to focus attention on the unique financial and educational needs of inner-city children. Title I of the Elementary and Secondary Act of 1965 had a special concern for providing financial assistance to low income schools.

Bottom (1970) pointed out that despite the massive aid to inner-city schools, far too many of the special programs lacked imagination and the quality necessary to overcome the educational handicaps created by a long history of deprivation. It can be added to Bottom's comments that many of these programs failed because they simply did not receive the support from the individuals in power to keep them operating for low income groups.

There are presently some special funds being appropriated to support educational programs in inner-city schools. While these special funds play a role in the general budgetary issues facing a school district, the major thrust of this discussion is on the way in which the resource picture is viewed by the teachers in the school.

The classroom teachers are among the first people to feel the press related to limited support funds. After all, they are ultimately responsible for implementing the program at the grassroots level, and the federal, state, and local budgetary procedures can appear far away when you are working with limited supplies and equipment in a classroom of 25-35 children. In addition, the age of some of our inner-city schools means that the limited space and facilities are further highlighted when there are no funds for modifying the environment.

The resource problems identified by the teachers in this study reflect their "here and now" need for receiving those services that will make the school a more productive place for them and the children. The problems that follow range from human resource issues to supplies and building repair.

1. There are insufficient support personnel.

2. The physical plant is inadequate; not enough special facilities.

3. There is insufficient clerical support for teachers.

4. There are inadequate equipment and supplies for varied programs.

5. School is in poor repair.

The strategies suggested for handling these problems reflect the fact that teachers believe in taking some initiative in the face of limited resources. Thus, the teachers utilized personal contact with parents, administrators and outside agencies to secure their needs.

PROBLEM: There are insufficient support personnel.

STRATEGIES:
    1.   Teacher involves parents:

Techniques Reported For This Strategy

Contact parents: call or make home visits.

Encourage parents to come in; participate in activities.

Ask parents to take child to clinic; use community services.

Confer with parent making suggestions for correction of problem.

Parents come as volunteers.

Teacher handles problem herself; teacher and child write contract that requires parent visitation.

    2.   Teacher involves students:

Have conferences and class meeting with kids.

Individually work with children (prep and lunch periods).

Give things they can accomplish.

Correct them in a positive manner.

Individualize program by games, SRA kit, talking alphabet so kids experience success in varied ways.

    3.   Teacher involves students, students assume some responsibility:

Make contracts for daily or weekly behavior goals.

Employ student tutors: high school, college, others.

Kids help; give weekly tests; do worksheets.

Work with individual while others do seat work.

Set up independent centers where they go work or pursue own interests.

Use children to exert peer influence to make less secure feel more secure.

Give special lessons for non-English speakers.

4. Teacher involves community, agencies, parent groups:

Use volunteers in the school to come to my class.

Get resource people involved in classroom activities where support is lacking.

Have kids tested at General Hospital for specific physical or emotional problems.

Had to find clinics where I could send my kids.

Go to Community Center myself to get available clothing for a child.

Send slow reader group to community reading assistant.

5. Teacher involves administration, other teachers, school personnel:

Involve teachers: advice, conferences, share materials, teaching responsibilities.

Involve administration: principal, assistant principal—advice, materials, support: grade chairman—coordinates parent assistance.

Utilize support personnel for ideas, materials: nurse, psychologist, social worker, director.

Consult child's folder.

Aide help: takes child and parent to clinic.

6.	Teacher assumes responsibility:

Do it myself: counseling, plan reading programs (means you work harder—be more competent).

Set up open communication relationship; use problem box.

Involve outside specialists: optometrist, social worker, psychologist.

Use heterogenous lesson grouping with two teachers moving from group to group.

Rely on own ingenuity, resources (example: when to call mother to pick up sick child).

Use student teachers.

Take students to clinics myself.

For child from shelter, keep in touch with shelter.

Find and bring in people who will do it.

Use extra materials rather than buy books for students performing below grade level.

Get ideas from current periodicals; outside course books.

Find information on my own; look for schools that handle various problems.

Contact people myself to help: friends.

Means you have to be a more competent and better teacher in class.

Got own reading aids: buy, make brings.

Compare my progress in room with other rooms at same level.

Devote more time to individualizing programs.

7. General statements:

Try to not be afraid to ask for help and advice.

PROBLEM: The physical plant is inadequate; not enough special **facilities.**

STRATEGIES:
1. Teachers bring in or find supplemental materials; plan activities:

Techniques Reported For This Strategy

Use big table as science lab.

Projectors, viewers.

Record player, tape recorder.

Library.*

Puppet stage.

Pupils make own materials.

Use living things (plants, fish, animals).

Put paper on chalkboard so film strips can be shown.

Set up own science experiments.

Set up folders with contracts and materials for each child.

Converted liquor store animated display into solar system.

Make special visual aids.

Set up learning centers in my own room:

    Listening, language, art
    Reading
    Math

     Art
     Science
     Use films
     Trips
     Set up tutoring or extra work stations.

2. Teacher involves parent:

Organized parents and they are builiding us a playground with money they raised themselves.

Inform parents of inadequacies so they can pressure principal or area supervisor.

Parents helped paint classroom.

3. Teacher involves students, students assume some responsibility:

Students bring in things for science (wire, batteries).

Students earned money for couch, lamps, and rugs for reading center.

Students built comfortable furniture; make bulletin board.

4. Teacher's techniques:

Class used for multiple activities; do everything in room.

Rearrange furniture; get rid of excess furniture; use screen for dividers to set up lab.

Turn class into home-like environment.

Teachers cooperate by doing activities on physical need basis; one sets up one thing, another something else.

Use teacher facilities (stove).

Must play only quiet games in class.

Let bigger boys sit at my larger desk.

118

Skip lessons requiring equipment I can't get.

Use pictures instead of a projector.

Use other space outside classroom; cloakroom, lunchroom, spare crafts room, vacant rooms.

Use community facilities: parks, recreation centers, churches, corporation facilities.

Make field trips: walks, play outside, to snow, sport events.

Teacher buys or makes herself: furniture, rugs, materials.

Teacher brings herself: furniture, rugs, materials.

Borrow from other schools (administration doesn't know about this).

Use as much color as possible in room.

5. Other strategies:

Brought superintendent to school to see problems.

Faculty and union complained to board.

Students eat with us.

Complain to principal about lack of facilities.

6. General statements:

Make do with what I have; improvise.

PROBLEM: There is insufficient clerical support for teachers.

STRATEGIES:
1. Teacher involves students:

Techniques Reported For This Strategy

Students do some attendance and filing, lunch count, monthly reports, correct each other's papers, bulletin boards.

2. Teacher involves other teachers, aides, administration:

Try to get help from secretary, clerks; be nice and polite.

Have clerical staff order supplies.

Aide helps me.

Go to grade chairman, supervisor, or teachers for advice.

Have other teachers help if not too busy; see what they do.

Administration posts daily what items are due.

3. Teacher does it herself:

Do on own time, come early, stay late, weekends, free days, lunch.

Do it myself; do own typing, Xeroxing, phone calls, cumulative folders, records.

Take it home.

Do work during prep periods.

Have built up file of material masters.

Constantly check with office regarding supplies that have not been sent.

Stay away from using dittos so I don't have to run them off.

Take time to really know where things are.

Take attendance as students enter room.

Tell clerical workers they must wait for records.

4. Other strategies:

Friends and relatives help.

Speak up at union meetings in favor of relief periods.

Teacher assists with formalizing plans for field trips.

5. General statements:

Let administration know I don't think I should do clerical work.

If you plan weeks ahead, there is support.

PROBLEM: There are inadequate equipment and supplies for varied programs.

STRATEGIES:
1. Teacher involves parents:

Techniques Reported For This Strategy

Parents bring in materials or loan equipment (sewing, cooking).

Invite parents into class as cooperating resource.

Ask parents to sponsor projects to raise money.

Appeal to parents who have businesses.

Parents bring in blue chip stamps; we use to buy equipment.

Parents attend weekly board meetings with teachers and make proposals.

2. Teacher involves students:

Children have fund raising drives.

Children bring in magazine clippings, physical education equipment.

Children bring in or buy equipment or supplies.

Children make materials for themselves: games, maps.

Children produce newspapers at $5.00 per subscription.

Children go to public library.

Children listen to evening newscasts.

Encourage pupils to appreciate things and to thank me.

Tell pupils to buy newspapers, weekly readers.

3. Teacher involves community, agencies, parent groups:

Get donations or available free materials from stores, church, community (inner tubes), foundations, publishers, universities.

Get materials from Title I funds.

PTA buys some materials.

Library provides some resources for us.

Obtain free materials from museum.

Community and teachers jointly made and presented proposal to Board of Education and Associate superintendent.

4. Teacher involves administration, other teachers, other schools:

Teachers borrow, share, cooperate in scheduling rooms together.

Constantly request: principal, board members, district office, resource teacher, grade chairman, curriculum teacher, supervisor.

Ask psychologist about more money.

Take equipment and supplies from other schools that have been closed.

Class is a pilot for special programs and is given supplies and equipment because of this.

Go to custodian.

Get equipment from school without administration's knowledge.

Try to influence budgeting.

Aides help make materials.

Engage in school activities to raise money.

Complain.

5. Teacher assumes responsibility:

Buy my own: recorder, record player, film strip, projector; spend $10-$15/week for pencils, magazines, spend $200-$600/year, $10/month if I think it will help the kids.

Improvise; make my own materials; use scrap lumber, junk.

Make games, puzzles.

Visual aids, charts.

Make or buy own materials for math.

Make or buy own materials for reading.

Experience stories used as readers.

Ditto pages of books I rip up, Xerox.

Use magazine clippings.

Rent things myself.

Take things around school that people don't use.

Bring in materials and equipment.

Run off materials where a friend works.

Plan programs around equipment availability; substitute; use less costly programs; make up original programs.

Sign up for audio-visual equipment far in advance.

Run off materials from a workbook series.

Borrow from various university resources.

Look beyond what is available at my school.

Get from relatives and friends.

Scrounge around the school.

Send out letters to get free magazines.

Sell subscription to our newspaper and sell papers.

Do library research; use library books.

Spend class money.

Find obsolete books and workbooks no one is using.

Give afternoons off while I make needed things.

Utilize other resources: attend workshops; get ideas from mini-courses, periodicals.

Participate in union insurance program which has good ideas for activities.

6. General statements:

Look for funding.

Make do with what you have; ration.

Publicity has helped increase community awareness of inadequate supplies; increased donations.

Decide what we need and find way to get it.

Do without if I can't get elsewhere (buy).

Don't give up.

PROBLEM: School is in poor repair.

STRATEGIES:
1.   Teacher involves students:

Techniques Reported For This Strategy

Get kids to take care of things.

Encourage pupils to clean up after themselves; form cleanup committees.

Decorate with help of class: painted class, put up curtains, pictures, children's artwork.

Do minor repairs and build things with the pupils.

Discuss condition in class and how to fix minor repairs.

Make use of space we have and keep it in good condition.

2.   Teacher does it herself:

Dust, clean, paint (clean our own windows before holidays).

Install shades and cover windows when shades are broken.

Procure tools from janitor and fix myself (broken bookcase or window).

Installed carpet in an area of classroom.

Making best possible use of what's there.

Bring in buckets of water because sinks don't work.

Rally support of other teachers.

3.   Teacher goes to administration, community, or parent groups:

Tell custodian/maintenance to repair windows, shades, sinks, etc.

Report to administration (principal, superintendent, nurse, etc.).

Make community aware through home visits.

Invite parents to school so they can see disrepair.

Fathers sometimes offer to repair broken items in rooms.

Try to get parent advisory group to school to pressure administration and board.

Had superintendent come view bathrooms/visit class.

Have petitioned for repairs.

4.   Other strategies:

Don't let children play in area where not safe.

I think my children were the ones vandalizing my room so I had to build better rapport before things improved.

Take trash can and put it under leak in the ceiling.

Wear our coats all day when it's cold.

Clearly, classroom teachers are not unaware of the larger resource problems faced by their school district. They are, however, more focused on those issues and problems they must face in carrying out the demands of an instructional program. In the daily press of the teaching load, it is not unusual for teachers to feel an immediate need for additional support personnel and to realize that a building which is too small or in need of repair tends to retard the program for the children.

Given the financial problems that individial schools and districts have reported during the last decade, it is no wonder that teachers feel that they must, through their professional organizations, play a greater role in budgetary matters which extend beyond their salary. The larger problems of budget and resources have been and will continue to be debated and negotiated by the school boards and professional groups. While discussions are proceeding on the higher levels, school administrators would be well advised to involve the professional staff and community in the distribution of the funds allocated to the local school. Such a cooperative effort would bring to light some of the problems faced by teachers and parents. Equally important, however, both groups will be able to bring their strategies and input into the shaping of the educational and budgetary programs.

CHAPTER VII

CLASSROOM MANAGEMENT PROBLEMS

The classic picture painted of inner-city schools by some of the professional literature and media sources is that they are full of a great deal of interpersonal conflict and hostility. While it would be inconsistent to deny the presence of some conflict, it is important to understand that many of the problems faced by the inner-city teacher are prevalent in suburban schools and a variety of teacher environments. Further, the teacher in the green grass areas of suburbia or the asphalt areas of the inner-city will need to tailor his or her classroom management strategies to recognize the background and needs of the children being served.

As we look at the question and issues related to classroom management, it is significant to first review the concept as a frame of reference for considering the views of the teachers in this study. Strom (1966) indicated that there is a positive aspect of classroom management where there is a kind of discipline that creates an order within which productive learning activities can take place with flexibility and freedom. Johnson and Bany (1970) define desirable classroom management as the process of organizing and coordinating the willing efforts of children to achieve their own educational objectives. This process requires selecting and using the means appropriate to the nature of the management problem and the situation in which it occurs. Using the Johnson and Bany framework, there appears to be a distinct pattern of activities by which teachers establish and maintain conditions whereby individuals in the classroom can be involved in bringing their talents to the educational tasks. Such a cooperative frame of reference of teacher-student interaction has some implications for classroom management in the inner-city school.

129

Classroom management in the inner-city school and any school will require the development of an effective classroom organization and a predictable system of relationships. It should involve the selecting of the method appropriate to the situation where problems arise which affect the functioning of the class organization. It must be kept in mind that the concepts related to classroom management should involve more than merely establishing a cooperative work group, satisfactory working conditions, and coordinating efforts toward predetermined objectives. The real meaning of the concept must also be used to indicate management activities that help to maintain the system and restore it when unresolved problems threaten the group or cause individual students to react in disruptive ways.

It is the management aspect of teaching that involves creating, establishing, and maintaining a classroom environment that encourages the release of human potential thereby enabling children to work together in classroom groups, to perform effectively, and to efficiently attain educational objectives in both the affective and cognitive domains.

Many of the management problems occurring and reoccurring in the inner-city classroom are naturally related to perception, sensitivity, conduct, and strategies of the teachers. The teachers in this study identified a variety of classroom management problems covering the following areas:

1. Pupils have little self control.

2. Corporal punishment is condoned in this school.

3. School expectations with regard to manners and social behavior are not sufficiently consistent with students' background.

4. There are too many unnecessary rules in this school.

5. Teachers and pupils have different values about profanity, sex, and aggression.

6. School rules demonstrate a lack of confidence in the students and are generally demeaning.

7. Pupils steal from one another.

8. Pupils don't have sufficient respect for authority.

9. Pupils fight with one another and are hostile and aggressive.

Professional educators have always developed a system of descriptors for indicating the behaviors manifested by children. The educational assumptions associated with the identified problems form the base for now reviewing the strategies the teachers employed to solve their management problems.

PROBLEM: Pupils have little self-control.

STRATEGIES:

1.   Teacher involves parents:

     Techniques Reported For This Strategy

     Send letters and notes home to get signed; call parents; ask for advice; inform of good or bad behavior; contingency contracts with parents.

     Go to visit parents at home.

     Invite parents into class.

2.   Teacher involves students:

     Permit class to make class rules with me.

     Students have weekly meetings; they decide on seating, work contracts; they learn that control is necessary in order to accomplish anything.

     Counsel individual child; "what we can do about it."

     Conduct class discussions when it interrupts the class.

     Use specific examples to students.

3.   Teacher as an authority:

     Make class standards explicit to students; teacher is "boss."

     Follow specific procedures in class when disruptive; e.g., turn off lights, have them put their heads down.

     Break up disputes, get students to "cool off."

     Keep fight-prone students separated.

4.   Teacher punishes:

     Use isolation.

Use standard procedures; demerits, extra work.

Restructure child's/group activities; e.g., recess, gym.

5. Teacher's personal approach:

Give positive reinforcement to child; e.g., praise, respect.

Have high expectations of child; stress independence.

Use peer pressure; teacher's personal contact outside of schoolroom.

Ignore some misbehavior.

6. Teacher's techniques:

Use outlets such as games, tape recorder, typewriter.

Use small groups of children; team learning; Glasser approach.

Use behavior modification methods; fight contracts.

Assign individual tasks to students; work contracts.

Counteract confusion in class with work; much personal interaction before and after class time.

Promote successful experiences for child.

Reward children for working toward set goals; e.g., good behavior merits, special privileges, prizes.

Have special seat arrangements; more open space; face away from one another; keep uncontrollable pupils close to me.

7. Teacher involves community, agencies, parent groups:

Work with social workers, psychologists of community centers; involve parents and children.

8. Teacher involves other teachers, principal, administration:

Seek principal's aid.

Seek other professional aid; psychologists, specialists.

9. General statements:

Get students to control and respect themselves.

Instill pride and motivation in students.

Counsel my students; reason with them to discourage fighting; be consistent.

Organize a microcosm, small community, something to call their own.

PROBLEM: Corporal punishment is condoned in this school.

STRATEGIES:
1. Carefully identify all of the official policy related to corporal punishment and examine your own views on the subject before considering its use.

2. Teachers report alternatives to corporal punishment:

Reason with the child or children (use of group discussions included) to find the source of the problem, discuss how it could have been avoided.

Give child more attention.

Ignore problem at times.

Make child feel badly by showing dislike for his behavior with looks, words, voice tone.

Have parents assist at home.

Send child to penalty room during recess.

Talk to parents at beginning of the year and ask them what they would like me to do.

Set up rules with children.

Isolate child from the class in order to give him/her a choice to work on problem and for use of individual counseling by teacher.

Provide an interesting program for learning.

Keep child out of special activity or take away privileges.

Use positive reinforcement for acceptable behavior.

Give extra assignments.

Stay after school or during recess.

Let child beat on playdough to work out aggression.

Have them write out why they've done what they've done.

3. Other strategies:

Afternoon discussions on behavior modification with other teachers.

Take child to the principal or vice principal.

Guidance counselor takes care of the big problems.

Tell other teachers to handle problem themselves; explain to parents how and why I handle children the way I do and I listen to them.

PROBLEM: School's expectations with regard to manners and social behavior are not sufficiently consistent with students' background.

STRATEGIES:
1.   Teacher seeks to change inconsistent rules:

Techniques Reported For This Strategy

Confront the administration to change rules.

2. Teacher seeks to get students to accept inconsistent rules:

Principal talks to parents to explain school policy.

Get students to line up after recess.

Talk to students about reasons for rules.

Relate acceptable and unacceptable social behavior of school to that of home to students.

Tell students they must abide by school rules.

Set an example of good manners.

Role play with and without manners; students choose preference of role to be played.

Class discussions about ways to show good manners.

Talk about mutual respect of rights of people.

Have child follow certain rules.

Contact parent of misbehaving child.

Use school guidance counselor.

Discourage aggression in students.

Get to know parents; when children find out they behave better.

Don't condone cursing.

Taught students to wash hands before eating.

Get students to use formal language in class; can use informal language out of school.

Ignore bad behavior; praise good behavior, manners, etc.

Punish kids for misbehavior.

Play up social gratitudes in lessons and units.

Have movies and books on manners and making friends.

3. Teacher seeks to compensate or counteract schools' expectations:

Tell students to avoid certain teachers whom they may provoke.

Tell other teachers why children act in certain ways; that they should adapt to children; approach children in their style.

Accept my students for what they are.

Have punching bag; child can vent frustrations here.

Set up consistent standards for students to follow.

Have pupils set up standards.

Evaluate personally without regard to school's expectations.

Give students physical fitness program.

Physically rearrange class; give children freedom of movement.

Give pupils high interest, relevant problem-solving work such as ecology, drug problems, work with low vocabulary stress.

Intercept referrals of other teachers to talk to pupils before they go to principal.

We as a class come to a median point of what manners should be.

Use informal language in class.

Don't attend assemblies where certain behavior is expected.

Treat other teachers and pupils with respect.

Talk about fighting (not in the sense that it's bad) and what is on their minds.

Give parties, programs, and talent shows in my home.

Have class discussions on similarities and ifferences of people.

Don't make pupils apologize for their actions; rather ask if they know why they acted that way.

Make students aware of my expectations.

Counsel children individually in my home.

Let children know you can communicate despite backgrounds; develop trust.

Respond as parents would.

Make child feel competent in class ("I can" approach).

Give kids alot of in-class responsibility.

Emphasize inter-classmate respect.

PROBLEM: There are too many unnecessary rules in this school.

STRATEGIES:
1.   Teacher tries to change rules:

Techniques Reported For This Strategy

Work together as a faculty seeing which rules work, and if they don't we call children in to discuss them.

Go to administration and challenge them; they go to school board and challenge them.

Go to other teachers and discuss it.

Go to community and discuss it.

2. Teacher explains need to accept and understand rules:

Explain to pupils why we have rules and live by them.

Have pupils create environment so their behavior conforms to rule without being aware of rules.

Uphold and abide by school rules.

Allow children to make class rules without bounds of school rules.

3. Teacher ignores existing rules or creates alternate rules:

Before school, permit kids to wander around my room (school has a rule which forbids wandering around halls before school).

Have two class rules: don't hurt anyone and don't interfere with another's learning.

4. Other strategies:

Tell kids not to go to other floors (there are different rules there).

PROBLEM: Teachers and pupils have different values about profanity, sex, and aggression.

STRATEGIES:
1. Teacher involves students:

Techniques Reported For This Strategy

Teacher tries to get children to conform to certain standards.

Discourage fighting in classroom and on school grounds.

Let student know my feelings and why profanity shouldn't be used in class; when, where to be used; set an example.

139

Contact parents.

Break up fights and ask why they fought.

Remind students of more appropriate words; discourage profanity.

Stress school rules.

Use peer pressure.

Isolate aggressive child; send to another room.

Distract child; get him interested in other things.

Praise kids for good behavior, token reinforcement.

Expel child from school.

Give them a stern "don't do it again" look.

Take away privileges from child.

Have child write "I will not. . . ."

Take children aside; discuss situation (bullying, profanity,
fighting).

Tell students one's body is his own and that nobody can
touch it unless we want them to.

Have children look up words in the dictionary.

Role play situations regarding aggression.

Explain to kids that sometimes a hit is accidental; all you
have to do is say "excuse me."

Discuss, read books, see films about getting along with
others.

Ignore it; don't comment, respond.

Demand respect at beginning of year—show love for pupils.

Make lesson out of aggressive act.

Tell pupils I won't tolerate aggression.

Send child to vice principal or administration.

Teacher aide handles problems of aggression.

Prevent aggression by lining kids up alphabetically.

Send child to guidance counselor for help.

2. Teacher employs cooperation and coexistence approach:

Talk to child to find out why he uses profanity and/or what frustrates him.

Don't write all things down on child's record.

Correct child casually.

Accept and respect student's value system.

Don't knock child's energy and enthusiasm; redirect it into child's schoolwork.

Openly discuss; have books about sex with class.

Let pupils know I curse; but don't do it in school.

Have team activities to get kids together.

Ask for mutual respect.

Integrate my views with those of students; we as a group agree on what norms would be.

Let children set up rules themselves.

Set up my own standards in my room.

Try to make child responsible for his actions.

Let children settle their own things, apologies, etc.

3. Other strategies:

Minischool has relaxed atmosphere (less fighting).

Have animals in class (lots of births and matings); gives kids a natural attitude about sex.

Talk to parents to discover their values.

University research group visits class one week for the purpose of improving group relations.

Glasser-type encounter groups between teachers and kids.

Let older teachers know language doesn't bother me.

Point out to other teachers expression of value system differences by kids.

Discipline committee at school gives teachers advice.

Act out our aggressions.

Advise teachers to join group sessions to discuss problems.

If you are a white teacher, try to understand black child's circumstances.

Set up revolving activities so pupils don't have to stay at any one thing.

Take pupils to park once a week to run around, burn off energy.

PROBLEM: School rules demonstrate a lack of confidence in the students and are generally demeaning.

STRATEGIES:

1. Teacher seeks to change rules:

   Techniques Reported For This Strategy

   Discuss rules with parties involved (kids/parents) and administration.

   Have student council where students can change rules.

   Go to community/parents; try to change rules.

   Teachers change rules in faculty meetings.

2. Teacher works for student acceptance of rules:

   Use myself as an example; role play situations; modeling.

   Tell students to be responsible so rules don't have to be imposed.

   Tell students: rules not set out of lack of confidence in students, but when broken, there's a way to take care of it.

   Tell students we've got to "work together," cooperate.

   Tell students we can't change rules, play the game.

   Let kids know when they've done a good job on something.

   Build up the pupils' confidence.

   Tell student I'll enforce a bad rule and why.

   Let those with good manners do special duties (set example for others).

   School squad aids in showing acceptable behavior.

3. Teacher tries to compensate or counteract rules:

   Ignore or do not enforce those I feel are not important or are demeaning.

Admit to student that some rules are "silly;" honesty important.

Let child set up his guidelines and/or own working program.

Set up minischool apart from rest of school.

Let students set up standards within a framework; give them leeway to develop independence and responsibility.

Give students job of responsibility (errands, etc.).

Instill trust in children (leave room for up to one hour).

4.   Other strategies:

Take the pupil's side when rule broken — find out real meaning of rule from originator/enforcer.

PROBLEM: Pupils steal from one another.

STRATEGIES:
1.   Teacher involves parents:

Techniques Reported For This Strategy

Contact parents, call (if stealing persists); notes returned with parent's signature; call parent and talk to them about problem.

2.   Teacher involves students; students assume some responsibility:

Class decides what should be done to person who steals; set up four-man jury; group decisions; whole class looks for item.

Child himself must deal with problem; child picks his own punishment; make child totally responsible; peer pressure takes care of it.

3.   Teacher discusses, explains:

144

Discusses alone with child who steals: don't make a big deal out of it but let him know I don't expect it to happen again; talk after school; ask how he'd like it to happen to him; what he thinks of it; ask them what's happened; ask him why he does it; ask child to return item; apologize.

Discuss with class: whole class discusses problem; how we would feel if their things were taken; point out good examples in class; ask first if you want something; respect for other's property; discuss responsibility for each other; discuss rules and reasons for them.

4. Teacher as an authority:

Teacher tells children how to protect their things: Don't bring valuables to school, or leave in desk; be responsible for own things; put identifying marks on their items; don't loan out anything valuable; monitor each other; no blame; no reward for return of article.

Tell child stealing is wrong; moralize with examples: "things belong to you, things belong to me;" "give it back." Make kids feel stealing is the worst thing you could do, put fear in their hearts; tell them I just don't accept stealing.

Teacher tells with specific limits: if pupils fight over a pencil, I take it away until someone needs it; things in class are for classroom use only; threaten kids with going through their desks if article doesn't show up; have children show the insides of pockets and purses; teach kids how to borrow; tell them to leave school materials at school; stop everything until stolen item is found; give new pencil to other child.

5. Teacher punishes:

If whole class is involved, no one goes home until someone admits to the stealing; threaten with no lunch period if item is not found; kids stay in room until property has returned; get student to confess; give time to return money.

Make children stay after school; take away privileges; threaten to call parents; make them stand in front of class and say why he stole.

6.   Teacher's techniques:

Talk about shoplifting and how they'd feel if people stole from them; try not to condemn those who steal as a mistake; I praise them for admitting they steal, I say something has been borrowed; never accuse until certain; no guilt placed, just return stolen article; don't make big deal out of incident; offer reward for returning lost property; ignore stealing of small items; they respect me, they steal less.

Tell student he's welcome to what I have; take money out of my own purse; deliberately leave my purse out to encourage a trusting atmosphere.

Give out pencils, textbooks, if they are missing; leave things around room with idea that everything in room is theirs; trust them; let them help themselves; let kids go into my desk for things they need.

Study on ecology or environment; discuss property related to animals; make comparisons to humans; read stories about how things belong to people.

Students work in teams; encourage sharing to eliminate stealing.

7.   Teacher involves other teachers, administration:

Send child to see principal or have him come to the room and talk to children/child; have principal talk to parent; call on assistant principal for suggestions; refer to other support staff.

8.   Other strategies:

Talk with students who have spent time in detention centers, camps, residential centers about why they had to go.

Tell students not to take class problems outside to their friends.

Encourage them; tell them I'm proud there hasn't been a problem; never any temptation; not a problem.

9.   General statements:

Encourage students to get along; try to set up atmosphere of caring; we talk about it; let them solve their own problems; tell students we all share the loss; things for everyone's benefit; find out who stole and make them return it.

Try to fill gap of personal need which causes child to want to steal.

Stress positive behavior; when it occurs, make a big deal out of it.

PROBLEM: Pupils don't have sufficient respect for authority.

STRATEGIES:
1.   Teacher involves parents:

Techniques Reported For This Strategy

Call or contact parents: get their support; ask them why child acts this way; what should be done about it; send notes home; parents make kids apologize to class.

Visit homes.

2.   Teacher involves student; student assumes some responsibility:

Children make rules with my help; class meetings where kids discuss problems and judge others' actions and make out disciplines or decisions; use logic or reason to establish expectations.

Let child assume authority position in the classroom.

Reward improved or positive behavior.

Get child to set own goals rather than child trying to please me; he works to please himself, no over-reaction to me, authority.

Whole class structure lends itself to fairness; we have frequent feedback self-evaluation on notion of earning respect and being responsible for own actions.

3.   Teacher discusses, explains:

Discuss mutual respect with children; mutual responsibility; ill effects of disrespect; develop trust level between teachers and students; get students not to fear you; show respect for my colleagues (aides, etc.).

Discuss authority figures: discuss who is authority at home and show that in school there has to be authority also; same with community authorities; discuss meaning of authority; problems person in authority has to go through; set examples for younger children; have kids examine teacher's role; all should be respected regardless of color; provide sane and flexible models of authority.

Teacher discusses with specific child; asks why he did certain thing; is it right? Ask him outside of earshot of others.

Teacher acts like a mother and tells them they must respond; reason with them about something that is wrong; discuss racial problems.

Try to explain reasons why we do things and why certain rules have to exist and why things I ask are necessary.

4.   Teacher as an authority:

Teacher demands respect: tell students to respect authority; property, each other, and be polite to adults; stress (in my room) that everyone respects me, that I am not their friend, and to call me Mrs.

Teacher exhorts responsibility: tell students they are responsible for themselves and others; if they don't listen, they won't learn; if they have criticisms, they should have alternatives; respect is earned.

Tell children I don't like their behavior and they are not to do it again.

5. Teacher punishes:

Teacher restricts child's activity: take away recess (playtime) and lunchtime, sometimes for the whole group; take away privileges.

Teacher sends child home, excludes from school until problem is corrected and parents respond.

6. Teacher's personal approach:

Teacher strives for consistency: try to be consistent; try to be reasonable, understanding; try to treat child fairly (firm but fair); don't put pupils down.

Teacher is approachable: tell pupils "I'm approachable;" respect them as human beings; address them by name; tell them more about me as human being; admit that I can be wrong, make mistakes.

Teacher gives special consideration: show my pupils I care for them; respect them; and go out of my way for them; give them attention. Compliment pupils (i.e., for backing up beliefs); stand up to principal; lay on line for pupils; don't accuse pupils, believe what they tell me.

Teacher facilitates understanding: asks child why he is hostile to me and other teachers; give him leeway to discuss problems with me; ask child if I've done anything to him; tell pupils I am here to teach them/to help them; talk to child when I see disrespect.

Teacher shows by example: show my respect for school authorities; act mean and ask students if they like me that way.

Use knowledge of community in lessons and stories.

Use instructional methods and techniques: cross-age tutoring, role playing.

7. Teacher involves other teachers, principal, administration:

Teacher seeks principal's aid: turn disrespectful child over to principal; principal/teacher set up conference for child.

Teacher seeks professional aid: go to guidance counselor; turn child over to home/school coordinator.

8. Other strategies:

   Teachers do not demand pupil respect: don't think students have to respect those bigger and older, don't have to show total obedience; ignore those teachers who try to enforce rules on kids; use token economy reward system (i.e., privileges).

   Role play, child assumes responsibility of teacher. I act as devil's advocate; I act as a child so child can see what I deal with (i.e., I hit other children, throw books on floor). Put child in authority position.

9. General statements:

   Get respect because of what I am; provide a type of framework which children can respect; don't put them down.

PROBLEM: Pupils fight with one another and are hostile and aggressive.

STRATEGIES:
1. Teacher involves parents:

   Techniques Reported For This Strategy

   Call, contact, talk to parents; explain how I handled situation and seek their advice. Determine if child is physically able for schoolyard combat.

   Invite, call parents into school; parents must see principal for child's re-entry after fight; parents are asked to pick up child who frequently fights.

2. Teacher involves student, student assumes some responsibility:

150

Make the student responsible for his actions; let the tough guy be a leader in class activities; have the two hash it out and make a decision about punishment.

Provide models using students who are tough, physically competent, and also cooperative.

Use group responsibility; students to discuss and evaluate the situation; children use peer pressure, sometimes mete out discipline; point out consequences of their actions.

3.   Teacher discusses, explains:

Discuss mutual respect and friendship with students.

Talk with child; find behavior related to problems at home.

Discuss need for self-control to child.

Discuss alternative solutions with child.

Help child see reasons and importance of getting along with his peers.

Discuss dynamics of fighting; role playing, films.

Write petitions as a class; get involved with community things, way to solve problems without violence.

Talk as a class about personal rights and responsibilities.

4.   Teacher as authority:

Separate or isolate combatants; calm them down; divert attention.

Prevent hostility; talk to pupils logically and ask, "did you understand what he meant?"

Mediate disputes; hear both sides; get to the bottom of it; make extensive use of witnesses.

Send rest of class out of the room; get students to shake

hands, apologize.

5.   Teacher punishes:

Take action myself; reprimand the child; keep after school; give extra work.

Restrict child's activities; take away breaks, privileges.

6.   Teacher's techniques:

Tell pupils about my experiences and give situations where you can't use violence; relate incidents in community where there has been violence.

Adapt work to level where they can achieve.

Use scientific inquiry; models of animals, younger kids; observe and analyze patterns of aggressive behavior.

Keep records of improvement; child keeps journal on daily feelings.

Use small group discussions.

Use drama techniques; theatrical games; role playing.

Have built-in flexibility; give kids freedom of choice; change student committees; offer individualized instruction.

Have special learning corners in the room.

Put problem child on different schedule so that he has less involvement with the other children.

7.   Teacher involves other teachers, principal, administration:

Seek principal's aid.

Seek assistant principal's aid and other professional support including aides and other teachers.

8.   Other strategies:

Try not to get outside people involved.

9.   General statements:

Talk about it; try to set up a group atmosphere; give them interesting things to do; don't expect them to sit in one place all day; make rules against fighting.

Explain to students that they can't solve all problems by hitting people.

Use universal standards, Golden Rule.

Use specific standards; threaten non-promotion.

Disapprove of fighting in class.

Try to channel aggressive behavior into socially acceptable behavior.

The comments from the previous section indicate that the problems associated with classroom management in the inner-city schools are very real for the teachers, and they must also apply to other school personnel. Real and challenging as these management problems may be, the professional is one who can develop productive programs for solving them. To this end, all techniques of classroom management depend on whether they are primary or secondary, whether they are used for student achievement or not, whether they act to stimulate learning or depress it, whether they respect the child's dignity as a human being or deny it (Clark, 1972).

At all times, the attitude and commitment of the teacher should be to create a classroom climate where optimal learning can take place for the inner-city child. This type of learning climate means that there is structure, form, and a standard of academic vigor in assignments which are aimed at helping the children to be competent persons in the total society. It also means that the climate clearly communicates to the children that they are respected for what they are and encouraged for what they can become. Building such a climate recognizes classroom problems, but it also attempts to capitalize on the strengths of the urban child in a school setting.

154

CHAPTER VIII

SUMMARY OF STRATEGIES FOR THE MOST PREVALENT PROBLEMS IN INNER-CITY SCHOOLS

Chapter I pointed out that the initial study from which this handbook was developed consisted of a compilation of the techniques and strategies reported by 248 teachers. Half of them were graduates of teacher training programs which focused on special preparation for inner-city schools, and the other half were "peer" teachers teaching in elementary schools in the same districts as the graduates.

The number of the responses given by the "peers" and graduates to specific strategy areas was not provided in the first section of the handbook. However, it was felt that these data were important for the end of the handbook in order to give the reader some summary views of the major strategies and techniques reported by the graduates and "peers," as well as some interpretive material gathered by the research staff.

Specifically, this final chapter will consist of: (1) an overall look at the number of strategies or techniques reported by graduate and "peer" teachers in each problem area, (2) a summary of the types of techniques graduates and peers reported using to handle the most prevalent problems, and (3) a list of those strategies or techniques that seemed unusual to the research staff who conducted this project; many of whom had teaching experience in urban schools.

1.   Summary of Reported Strategies and Techniques

A rough indicator of resourcefulness is the number of strategies and techniques teachers described. An overall look at the total number of techniques mentioned for each of the problem areas (see following table) revealed that with one sharply defined exception, the Colleague and School Staff Problem area, differences between graduates of exemplary training programs and their "peer" teachers were small.

Indicator of Resourcefulness: Number of Strategies and Techniques Itemized by Teachers to Cope with Problems in the Inner City

Problem Areas		Peers	Graduates
A.	Parent and Community Problems	899	980
B.	Instructional and Learning Problems	1,782	1,882
C.	Colleagues and School Staff Problems	443	719
D.	School Administration Problems	439	435
E.	Inadequate Resource Problems	381	369
F.	Affective and Classroom Management Problems	869	963
	TOTAL	4,813	5,348

The graduates reported many more methods than peers in the area of Colleague and School Staff Problems. A review of the specific techniques that teachers reported in this problem area[1] showed that graduates selected more techniques that engage others in personal involvement with other teachers, administrators, or parents with regard to prejudice, low morale, and lack of support or cooperation. Graduate teachers were particularly resourceful in dealing with the problem of low expectations other teachers had for pupils' performance.

In four other areas, graduates mentioned a slightly greater number of techniques than did peers. These areas included: (A) Parent and Community Problems, (B) Instructional and Learning Problems, (E) Inadequate Resources, and (F) Affective and Classroom Management Problems. While the areas of Colleague and Staff Problems (C), and

---

[1]See for example in Chapter IV.

School Administration Problems (D) are important factors to consider, they are not discussed in the following sections because there was only a small level of difference between the two group of teachers on these items.

2. Summary of the Four Most Prevalent Areas Identified By Graduate and Peer Teachers

In summary, there is a trend toward graduate teachers registering more techniques that reflect personal interaction with parents, teachers, and pupils. Peer teachers reported using methods of the same type, but they do not report them as frequently as graduate teachers. Graduates also reported a use of "personal" or "off the job" time more frequently than peers.

In short, teachers who felt highly competent overall tended to pick the same types of teaching techniques; graduates tended to name more methods and to choose those strategies which called for personal interaction more often than peers. In this connection, further studies would determine if greater personal involvement of the type described by the graduates enhances the learning environment of the pupil, and if this involvement provides the pupil with an expanded and enriched learning "space."

Summary Of Techniques For Most Prevalent Problems

Parent and Community Problems (Area A)

PROBLEM: Parents are unable to help their children with schoolwork because they lack educational opportunities.

TECHNIQUE: Teacher gives directions and materials to parents primarily through letters, notes, kits, directions, etc. and sends them home with child; she makes herself available to them by giving them her home phone number; she may phone them herself.

Teacher initiates home visits, conferences, and parent meetings at school to help parents understand homework, use of materials, books; teacher may involve or encourage parents in learning experiences of their own such as workshops or classes.

Teacher depends upon the student or other children to assume responsibility for the homework rather than the parent; or teacher works with children in the classroom during school hours or perhaps after school employing various methods of instruction.

Instruction and Learning Problems (Area B)

PROBLEM: There is not enough time to plan the curriculum.

TECHNIQUE: Time has been released for planning the curriculum; or the administration's or teacher's expectations for planning the curriculum has been changed to fit the time available.

Teacher seeks to meet present expectations for a planned curriculum using various techniques such as using their own free time, planning with other teachers, use of special guides, etc.

PROBLEM: Classes contain pupils of various ability levels.

TECHNIQUE: Teacher involves other teachers, personnel, administration, and parents for group and individualized attentions.

Teacher involves student and student assumes some responsibilities in classroom for peer tutoring, independent study.

PROBLEM: Pupils have difficulty thinking in abstract terms.

TECHNIQUE: Teacher involves parent groups, agencies, other teachers, and the community.

Teacher's techniques and materials designed to provide student with a learning experience with abstract concepts.

PROBLEM: Pupils often achieve below grade norm.

TECHNIQUE: Teacher involves other teachers, administrators, and parents for group or individualized learning experience.

Teacher's personal approach and techniques used to attempt to raise student's achievement.

Teachers ignore tests because they are not culture free.

PROBLEM: Too many pupils in the classroom.

TECHNIQUE: Teacher involves parents, community, other teachers, and administration to provide alternate classroom arrangements or learning experience.

Resource Problems (Area E)

PROBLEM: The physical plant is inadequate.

TECHNIQUE: Teacher provides activities and materials that she provides herself. Teacher attempts to compensate for inadequacies with improvisation and student involvement.

Teacher involves the parents or the administration in attempting to correct the inadequacies.

PROBLEM: There are inadequate equipment and supplies for varied programs.

TECHNIQUE: Teacher purchases equipment and supplies herself (or begs, borrows and steals, if necessary); teacher involves parents, children, other teachers in obtaining what she needs; teacher innovates with what she can get to compensate somewhat for inadequate equipment and supplies.

Constantly requests from administration, district office, others in power, for materials.

PROBLEM: There is insufficient support personnel.

TECHNIQUE: Teacher assumes some or all responsibility for that ordinarily shouldered or taken care of by support personnel.

Teacher seeks resource support personnel herself.

Affective, Classroom Management Problems (Area F)

PROBLEM: Pupils fight with one another and are hostile and aggressive.

TECHNIQUE: Teacher involves parents and/or involves the student either with discussions involving the entire class or with some form of student interaction.

Teacher intervenes, acts as an authority, and punishes the students involved.

Teacher employs special instructional methods, use of curriculum or classroom space.

Teacher involves principal, vice principal, counselors.

PROBLEM: Pupils have little self-control.

TECHNIQUE: Teacher involves community, agencies, parents, other teachers, principal, and resource people.

Teacher involves students in determining solutions.

Teacher punishes or acts as an authority.

Teacher's personal approach and techniques to self-control problems.

3. Summary of Unique Strategies From the Four Most Prevalent Areas

A review of the set of unique strategies suggests the same emphasis on the interaction process. Members of the project staff with former teaching experience in inner-city schools selected strategies or techniques according to what they considered "different" or "unusual." The project staff members made their selections without regard to graduate and peer differences. They tended to follow the pattern of the graduate teacher by identifying those strategies which more often involved an extended group of "others" in the education process. The staff consistently chose techniques where the teacher expanded the circle of significant others in the learning "space" of the pupils (e.g., peers, parents, community people, other teachers), involving them actively in decision-making, responsibility, and exposure. Other unique strategies identified by the staff required a degree of substantial personal commitment, innovation, and originality on the part of the teacher.

Unique Strategies For Most Prevalent Problems

Parent and Community Problems (Area A)

PROBLEM: Because parents lacked educational opportunity, they are unable to help their children with schoolwork.

UNIQUE STRATEGIES:

Set up study centers in homes and times for children to study at home.

Use games to involve both parent and child.

Workshops for parents.

Find out from the board of education what educational programs or materials are available for parents.

Have parent assistance club.

Cross-age tutoring.

Homework centers in the classroom for those who can't

161

do it at home.

Resource people include coordinating instructors, para-professionals, student teachers, community workers, college students, university field workers, and bilingual aides.

Instructional and Learning Problems (Area B)

PROBLEMS: Pupils often achieve below grade norm.
Too many pupils in the classroom.
Classes contain pupils of various ability levels.
Pupils have difficulty thinking in abstract terms.

UNIQUE STRATEGIES: (Applicable to all of the problems mentioned above)

Use of aides other than paraprofessionals, such as high school and college students and parents.

Faculty formed a minischool/open corridor structure with an open classroom (four classes, five teachers), subject matter derived among teachers in a team teaching situation.

Individualized instruction using such techniques as contracts, conferences, and activity rotation.

Children make their own work contracts.

Use manipulative games that provide feedback.

Parents sign learning contracts.

Cross-age, peer, and sibling tutoring; pupils who can't write/read have "secretaries" who know material and get credit for writing what nonwriter dictated.

Have group discussions on how communication affects others and how it influences what happens to them.

Incorporate abstract ideas (sadness, happiness) in reading.

Role play concerning abstract concept (prejudice).

Use fables, folklore, and fantasies, "imagine you are..."

Talk about feelings and self-concept.

Resource Problems (Areas E)

PROBLEM: There are insufficient support personnel (remedial specialists, counselors, consultants).

UNIQUE STRATEGIES:

Teacher handles problem herself; teacher and child write contract that requires parent visitation.

Teacher takes students to clinics herself.

PROBLEM: There are inadequate equipment and supplies for varied programs.

UNIQUE STRATEGIES:

Ask parents to sponsor projects to raise money.

Kids produce newspapers at $5 per subscription.

Community and teachers jointly made and presented proposal to board of education and associate superintendent.

Engage in school activities to raise money.

Several thousand dollars gathered among five teachers at first, and then $200, $10/month, in order to buy needed equipment.

PROBLEM: The physical plant is inadequate; not enough special facilities.

UNIQUE STRATEGIES:

Organized parents and they are building us a playground with money they raised themselves.

Students built comfortable furniture; made bulletin board.

Affective and Classroom Management Problems (Area F)

PROBLEM: Pupils fight with one another and are hostile and aggressive.

UNIQUE STRATEGIES:

Use group responsibility; students to discuss and evaluate the situation; children use peer pressure, sometimes mete out discipline; point out consequences of their actions; use a Glasser type approach.

Write petitions as a class; get involved with community things, ways to solve problems without violence.

Use scientific inquiry; observe and analyze patterns of aggressive behavior of animals; compare to behavior of humans.

Keep records of improvement; child keeps journal on daily feelings.

Use drama techniques; theatrical games; role playing.

Allow fighting, think aggression is good; accept some fighting.

PROBLEM: Pupils have little self-control.

UNIQUE STRATEGIES:

Students have weekly meetings; they decide on seating, work contracts; they learn that control is necessary in order to accomplish anything.

Develop contracts or agreements with students about fighting.

Which problems then were the most prevalent ones identified by inner-city teachers? According to the teachers in this study, the instructional/learning problems and problems arising from inadequate resources are the most prevalent problems they have to face. The teachers also stated that affective/classroom management problems are common areas of concern in our inner-city schools. These types of problems more directly affect teacher-pupil relations than those less frequently cited problems which concern relations with parents, community members, colleagues, school staff, and administrators.

Graduates of the "exemplary" or special programs aimed at inner-city teaching reported fewer problems than peer teachers with parents and community and with affective/classroom management. These differences may reflect the "exemplary" programs' emphasis on inner-city field experiences. Such experiences, for example, may help prepare teachers for life in the inner-city school and community. While it was not a major factor for consideration in the handbook, there were some differences between Black (N=78) and White (N=164) teachers in those problems relating to parents and community, instruction and learning, and colleagues and school staff (Black teachers gave fewer problems for these areas). It was felt that these differences in the perceptions of Black and White teachers indicated the need for different preservice training approaches depending on the trainee's background and prior experiences.

Finally, the reader might ask the meaning of all of these problems and strategies for his or her own teaching. This writer assumes this to be a valid issue for the reader to consider and in a number of ways an important stage of development after reading the book. After all, our teaching strategies for inner-city children in themselves must always be viewed with a question as to their value, and seen in a formative manner in terms of the need for them to be constantly improved. While the questions might emerge concerning the implications of the problems and strategies, and whether or not they were constructive or destructive, there should be little question about the need for inner-city children to have only those teachers who strive for teaching excellence and productive program offerings.

The children of the inner city, like their counterparts everywhere, need instructional programs that are solid in its content, humanistic in its concerns, and relevant to the social and cultural life of the child. In addition, the teachers and their curriculum should be broad enough to help the inner-city child to understand people in their environment and the total world. Such a program would recognize the problems and limitations of some inner-city children but also understand the positive aspects of their lifestyle.

We must build sound programs in our inner-city schools in spite of the fact that some of the children bring a multiplicity of problems to the school, the school budgets are sometimes too small, the parents often do not give us support, and the working conditions are tough. For in the final analysis, the inner-city children, White, Black, Brown, or Yellow, have many strengths along with their weaknesses, and the professional educators must be creative enough to remediate the weaknesses, to tap the strengths, and to unshackle their potential.

REFERENCES

Berry, G.L. Education in inner-city schools: Community challenge. *Journal of Black Studies*, 1973, *3*, 315-327.

Bottom R. *The education of disadvantaged children*. New York: Parker Publishing, 1970.

Clark, K.B. *A possible reality: Design for the attainment of high academic achievement for inner-city schools*. New York: Emerson Hall, 1972.

Cullum, A. *The geranium on the windowsill just died but teacher you went right on*. Chicago: Harin Quist Publishers, 1973.

Curtin, J. *Supervision in today's elementary schools*. New York: Macmillan, 1964.

Evaluative assessment of exemplary pre-service teacher training for inner-city elementary teachers: Inner-city teaching strategies. Contemporary Research Incorporated, Los Angeles, 1972.

Issues in school finance. 92nd Congress, 2nd session, Washington, D.C.: Government Printing Office, 1972.

Johnson, L.V. & Bany, M. *Classroom management: Theory and skill training*. New York: Macmillan, 1970.

Storm, R.D., (Ed.). *The inner-city classroom: Teacher behaviors*. Columbus; Charles E. Merrill, 1966.

Owens, R. *Organizational behavior in schools*. Englewood Cliffs, NJ: Prentice-Hall, 1970.

Pellergrino, J. Parent participation. *Education Canada*, 1973, *13*, 5-9.

Weaver, E.K. The new literature on education of the black child. In R. L.Jones (ed.), *Black Psychology*. N.Y.: Harper and Row, 1972.

Why do some urban schools succeed? Phi Delta Kappa Study of Exceptional Urban Elementary Schools. Bloomington, Indiana: Phi Delta Kappa, 1980.